TANKMASTER

An essential guide to choosing your

# TROPICAL

## FRESHWATER FISH

### GINA SANDFORD

INTERPET PUBLISHING

## Author

**Gina Sandford's** interest in fishkeeping began with
a goldfish and developed to include sticklebacks, young
perch, pike and eventually tropical fish. She has kept
and bred many species, but has a particular interest in
catfishes. She has written several books and
contributed many articles to magazines and journals.
Gina travels widely, giving audiovisual presentations and
lectures to both experienced and young audiences.

Published by Interpet Publishing,
Vincent Lane, Dorking, Surrey, RH4 3YX, England.
All rights reserved.
ISBN 13 -   978 1 902389 95 0
This reprint 2008

### Credits

Created and designed: Ideas into Print,
New Ash Green, Kent DA3 8JD, England.
Production management: Consortium, Poslingford,
Suffolk CO10 8RA, England.
Print production: Sino Publishing House Ltd., Hong Kong.
Printed and bound in China. This reprint 2005

*Below:* The guppy is
one of the more
flamboyant fish for
beginners. Its finnage
has been developed to
enhance its appeal,
but choose tankmates
with care because the
fins are also appealing
to fin-nippers!

# Contents

The fish are arranged in groups, but bear in mind that within some groups there are several families. The majority of cyprinids, characins, livebearers and anabantids are midwater-swimming fish that should be kept in shoals, pairs or trios. The catfishes and loaches are predominantly bottom-dwellers. The fish within the four remaining groups have slightly more specific needs and are recommended for fishkeepers with 6-12 months experience.

# UNDERSTANDING YOUR FISHES

The whole purpose of setting up your aquarium is to keep fish and, in this case, tropical freshwater fish. You will probably have gazed at the tanks in your local aquarium shop and decided which fishes you would like to keep. This book provides you with a selection of easy-care fishes, with guidance on the conditions they need to thrive in your aquarium.

Throughout the book we mention the names of fins and other parts of the body. The drawings here will help you understand what we are talking about. If you turn back to them every now and then the terms will soon begin to stick in your mind.

### The names and functions of the fins
The fins fall into two sorts: single and paired. Single fins are the dorsal, adipose (if there is one, not all fish have one), caudal and anal fin. The paired fins are the pectoral and ventral fins (also known as pelvic fins). Fish propel themselves through the water by making sinuous body movements and the fins keep the fish stable. (The caudal fin is used to provide initial thrust, but it is the S-shaped movements of the body that keep the fish mobile.) Some fish, such as cichlids, use their pectoral fins to make fine manoeuvres. Fins can be elongated, flamboyant structures that we can use to differentiate the sexes, but this is not always apparent on young fish.

In certain fishes, some of the fins are modified for other purposes. In male livebearers, for example, the supporting rays of the anal fin are fused to form a structure, known as the gonopodium, used for internal fertilisation of the female. Some fish, such as

catfishes, also have fin spines. These are used as protection against predators or they may be used for wedging the fish into crevices. The adipose is a strange fin composed of fatty tissue and it may or may not have a fin spine. Its function is not clear.

### Fish senses
Fish possess the usual range of senses. Eyes vary in size and position depending on the fish's lifestyle. Barbels around the mouth are well developed in some fish and enable them to touch and taste likely food items that may be in the gravel or silt on the bottom. (Some predatory catfish use their barbels to locate prey in midwater.) The nostrils are not used for breathing but let the fish smell at a distance. The sense of hearing is provided by an organ unique to fishes. This is the lateral line, a line of tiny pits that run along the flanks. These detect minute vibrations in the water and alert the fish to possible danger, the nearness of obstacles and the presence of food.

## Typical cyprinid (barbs, danios, rasboras, etc.)

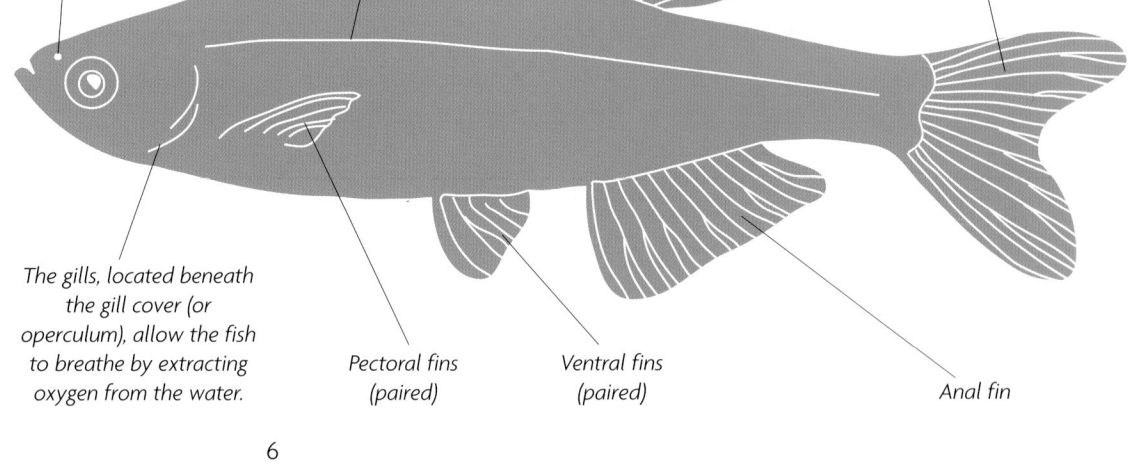

*Nostril*

*Lateral line*

*Dorsal fin*

*Caudal fin*

*The gills, located beneath the gill cover (or operculum), allow the fish to breathe by extracting oxygen from the water.*

*Pectoral fins (paired)*

*Ventral fins (paired)*

*Anal fin*

## Natural habitat

Fish can be found in most bodies of water around the world. The fish featured in this book are tropical, but this does not mean that they all require the same temperatures. Even in the tropics there are variations depending on altitude and type of habitat. Swift-flowing mountain streams are cool and highly oxygenated, whereas the lower courses of rivers can be sluggish and poorly oxygenated. Lakes have differing zones of temperature, while still pools can be very hot, very low in oxygen and may even evaporate. You need to take all these factors into account when keeping tropical fish in an aquarium at home and ensure that you keep them within their favoured range of conditions.

*Left: Swamps rich in insect life and small aquatic invertebrates make a wonderful habitat for some species of fish. The waters of this Florida swamp abound in mollies, livebearing fish ideal for the aquarium.*

## Typical armoured catfish

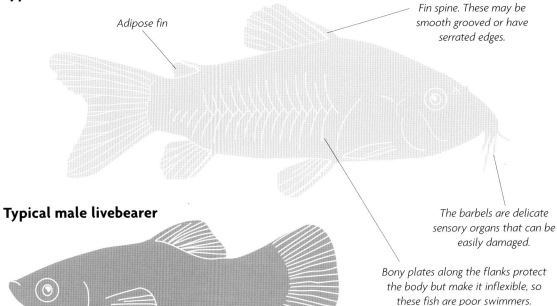

Adipose fin

Fin spine. These may be smooth grooved or have serrated edges.

*The barbels are delicate sensory organs that can be easily damaged.*

*Bony plates along the flanks protect the body but make it inflexible, so these fish are poor swimmers.*

## Typical male livebearer

Gonopodium (fused anal fin used for internal fertilisation).

## Origins

*These maps show where the fish lives in the wild. Some fish species have a very localised distribution, such as one river or lake, whereas other fish are found over a wide region.*

# COMPATIBILITY WITHIN THE AQUARIUM

Setting up a balanced community of fishes in an aquarium means taking into account the needs of a particular species as well as the compatibility between fish species. It is also vital to know what size of tank suits each fish and what regions they inhabit within the tank. Reading through the main text for each species will provide the information you need. Before you do that, here are some general points to take into account.

## The balance of fish in the aquarium

For each species we suggest the minimum number that you should keep in the smallest recommended aquarium. Some fish should be kept as single specimens, either because they fight with each other at the least provocation or they require a territory and there is insufficient space for more than one. Where fish can be sexed, then it is wise to buy a pair, but if they cannot easily be sexed then the minimum number may be just two. Many fish naturally live in shoals. You should keep shoaling fish in a shoal not simply because they look good but because this is how they live in the wild. Among the advantages of living in a shoal are protection from predators, a greater chance of finding a mate and more luck with finding food.

## Sizes of fish

The size of fish can be an important factor in the harmony of your aquarium community. Although a large fish can be quite peaceful, it may be too boisterous for smaller species. In extreme cases, smaller fish may be so intimidated that they stop

**Number of tropical fish to a tank**
*Surface area is the governing factor for the number of fish you can keep in an aquarium. For tropical freshwater species you need 75 sq cm (12 sq in) of surface area per 2.5cm (1in) body length (do not include the tail) of fish. A tank measuring 60x30cm (24x12in) has a surface area of 1800 sq cm (288 sq in) and will hold about 60cm (24in) of freshwater tropical fish.*

**Right:** *A small shoal adds movement to the tank. These* Hemigrammus bleheri *have similar needs to cardinal tetras.*

*This 60x30cm (24x12in) tank has four fish, each measuring 15cm (6in) long, which together add up to the maximum carrying capacity of 60cm (24in) of fish body length.*

*This 60x30cm (24x12in) tank has 12 fish, each measuring 5cm (2in) long, which together add up to the maximum carrying capacity of 60cm (24in) of fish body length.*

feeding and die. On the other hand, a fish is as safe as the size of its mouth! An angelfish may have grown up with a shoal of neon tetras and no harm has ever come to either party. When the neons die of old age and small replacements are introduced, however, they may disappear one by one down the throat of the angelfish! You cannot blame the angel, it is simply doing what comes naturally – eating something that is small and looks like food.

It has long been believed that large species will not grow to their full size if you keep them in a small tank. This is not so. With modern filtration systems, you can easily maintain good enough conditions for the fish to keep growing. Indeed, it has been known for fish to grow to such a size that they are restricted in the aquarium to the point where they are unable to turn around.

## The importance of territory

Territorial behaviour can be a dominating influence in the aquarium. Although a tank may seem to be quite large to us, to the fish, it is small. Those that have grown up together in one aquarium have worked out their territories and, if you watch them carefully, you will see that each one has a set pattern of going round the tank. If you add a new fish to a tank that has been established for many months or even years, mayhem can ensue. A simple solution is to move a couple of rocks around so that you dismantle the established territorial boundaries and all the fish have to start again. Choosing fish to occupy the various levels in the tank helps to alleviate territorial problems.

**Fish measurements**

*The sizes of fishes given throughout the book refer to the length of the body, excluding the tail fin.*

*Above: Lurking at the water surface, the sparkling panchax (Aplocheilus lineatus) is ideally placed to snap up any small insects that land on the water.*

## Levels in the aquarium

*The top layer of water to a depth of about 5cm (2in) is home to fish that swim and feed at the surface, such as the sparkling panchax (Aplocheilus lineatus).*

*The biggest zone in the tank is the middle layer, where you will find shoaling fish. such as neon tetras and other midwater swimmers.*

*Fish such as catfishes and loaches, will feel at home at the bottom of the tank.*

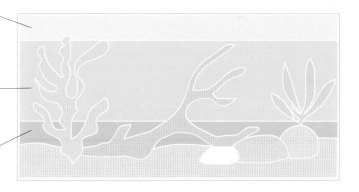

9

# TAKING CARE OF YOUR FISH

Fish function within certain environmental ranges and you must provide these if the fish are to remain healthy. Clearly, creating and maintaining the right water conditions is the single most important aspect of successful fishkeeping.

## The pH and hardness of aquarium water

The most important aspects of water quality are pH (ie whether the water is acidic, neutral or alkaline) and hardness, as these are the most difficult characteristics for you to alter. It is far better to live with the tapwater conditions you have available when you start out, because there are so many other new tasks and topics to divert your attention. Most of the fish described in this book will live in water

### What does the pH scale mean?

*The term 'pH' literally means 'potential Hydrogen' and reflects the relative number of hydrogen ions (H+) and hydroxyl ions (OH−) in the water. The more hydrogen ions there are, the more acidic the water. The more hydroxyl ions there are, the more alkaline the water. When they balance out, the water is neutral. The pH scale extends from pH0 (extremely acidic) to pH14 (extremely alkaline), with pH7 representing neutral. The scale is logarithmic, which means that a shift of one unit reflects a ten times change in the degree of acidity or alkalinity. You can use test kits, paper strips or an electronic meter to test the pH of tapwater or your aquarium water.*

### Measuring water hardness

*In the fish profiles we use terms such as 'slightly soft' and 'slightly hard' to describe the water hardness needed to keep your fish in peak condition. What scale do we use to interpret those descriptions more precisely? The most widely used units to measure water hardness are degrees of hardness (°dH). This table shows how that scale reflects those general descriptions and how it compares to another commonly used scale of milligrammes of calcium carbonate per litre of water, which is the same as parts per million (ppm).*

| Description | °dH | Mg/litre (ppm) $CaCO_3$ |
|---|---|---|
| Soft | 0-3 | 0-50 |
| Slightly soft | 3-6 | 50-100 |
| Slightly hard | 6-12 | 100-200 |
| Moderately hard | 12-18 | 200-300 |
| Hard | 18-25 | 300-450 |
| Very hard | over 25 | over 450 |

with a pH value between 6.5 and 7.5 (ie somewhere around the neutral value of 7.0) and that is slightly soft to slightly hard. The majority of community aquariums seem to run perfectly well within these parameters. (See the panels for a more detailed description the pH and hardness scales.)

## The temperature of the water

The next parameter to look at is the temperature of the water and this is something you can adjust quite easily. Look at the ranges for all the fish you wish to keep and see where the common ground is, then set your heater-thermostat accordingly. For example: swordtails, cherry barbs and bronze corydoras need temperature ranges of 21-28°C (70-82°F), 23-26°C (73-79°F) and 22-26°C (72-79°F) respectively. You could therefore keep them all in the range 23-26°C (73-79°F) and you should set your thermostat at, say, 24°C (75°F). This will give you a little leeway in both directions.

## The amount of oxygen in the water

Oxygen levels can also play an important part in providing healthy living conditions in the aquarium. You can adjust this relatively easily by increasing the amount of aeration by using an airpump and airstone or by fitting a form of filtration that creates agitation at the water surface. Since it is at the surface that oxygen enters the water and waste gases such as carbon dioxide leave it, agitating the water surface increases this exchange of gases.

## Regular maintenance

In the small closed system of an aquarium, things can go wrong quickly! Fortunately, this does not happen too often and you can prevent this by paying attention to regular maintenance.

This can be the most enjoyable part of fish-keeping because it allows you the time to watch and observe as well as do things. On a day-to-day basis, feeding and a general check that all the fish come out to feed is the most obvious regular activity. Avoid overfeeding – a hungry (but not starving) fish is a healthy fish. When you feed, check the temperature with a quick glance at the thermometer and also touch the tank. You'll be surprised at how quickly you get used to feeling the right temperature and this is useful if you break your thermometer!

You can also check whether your filter system is fully operational and if not, why not? Baskets on external power filters can clog quickly if a leaf from an aquarium plant becomes caught in them and swift removal will ensure the filter's efficiency.

Once every 10-14 days you will need to make a water change. This involves replacing 10-20% of the volume of the tank with new water at the right temperature. At this time, check that the filter is running properly and once a month change part of the filter medium in external filters, wash sponges in internal power filters or siphon the gravel in tanks with undergravel filtration systems.

These times are approximate depending on your aquarium. If you keep an aquarium log you will soon see a pattern developing for your system and this will help alert you to potential problems if things start to change.

## Health care

At some stage, your fish will fall ill. The main illnesses are whitespot, which is caused by a parasite, and fungal and bacterial diseases that occur as secondary infections. Injury, stress or a deterioration in living conditions can all be contributing factors. You can avoid these by careful maintenance and choice of fish. A simple water change and check on the filtration system can often cure a problem before it really starts. Should your fish fall ill, take time to diagnose the problem correctly before treating with a proprietary product. Follow the maker's instructions precisely when dosing the tank. Never mix remedies, as lethal concoctions can result.

**How the information panels work throughout the book**

*The basic requirements for keeping each species are given in an easy-to-read panel, such as the example shown below. Breeding details, if available, are provided as a separate text block.*

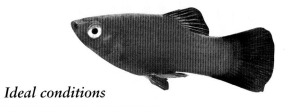

**Water quality**
*A guide to the range of water conditions the fish requires.*

**Temperature**
*This gives the range within which the fish lives.*

**Food**
*Guidance on the range of foods that the fish will accept. These are all commonly available.*

**Minimum number**
*You should keep at least this number in your aquarium to make the fish feel secure and at ease.*

**Minimum tank size**
*This is the minimum length of the aquarium you should use for a particular fish. Aquariums are available in a range of standard sizes, such as 60x30x30cm (24x12x12in) and 90x38x38 (36x15x15in).*

**Tank region**
*Some fish will swim at all levels in an aquarium, whereas others stay in particular zones most of the time. Use this information to set up a balanced aquarium with fish at all levels.*

## Ideal conditions

**Water:** Slightly acidic, slightly soft.
**Temperature:** 18-23°C (64-73°F).
**Food:** Small live or frozen aquatic invertebrates, such as daphnia, mosquito larvae and bloodworm. Flake foods. Green foods.
**Minimum number in the aquarium:** 2.
**Minimum tank size:** 60cm (24in).
**Tank region:** Bottom, middle and top.

## Breeding

Many of the fish profiles in this book feature a panel on how they breed in the aquarium. Many fishes lay eggs in the community aquarium, but the parents and other fish in the tank will eat them. To be successful with breeding, it is best to spawn the parents in a different, usually quite bare, tank and put them back in the community aquarium once they have laid their eggs. This leaves the young fish, or fry, to develop safely on their own. Some fishes, such as the livebearers, produce live young. Many of these young fish may survive in a community aquarium if there are plants in which they can seek protection.

FAMILY: CYPRINIDAE (BARBS)

This hardy little fish is ideal for beginners, as it is not fussy about water conditions (provided they do not become too warm) and will eat anything from algae and plants to flake, tablet and live foods. Rosy barbs are peaceful and tolerant of other species and mix well with other similar-sized barbs. They are constantly on the move, so arrange the plants to allow space for this.

Young stock will not show the beautiful colours of the adults but appear silvery gold. It is not until they begin to mature that the males take on the red hues and the females become a deeper golden colour. To ensure that you acquire both sexes, buy five or six youngsters or choose adult fish. If you want to see them at their best, be sure to keep both sexes so that the males display to the females.

### Other forms

*A long-finned form is available but it is more demanding. Keep the temperature towards the upper end of the range. Be sure to maintain water quality and do not overlook regular water changes.*

### ▶ Origins

*Streams, rivers and pools in northern India, Assam and Bengal.*

*The bright colours from which the rosy barb gets its common name develop as the fish matures.*

### ▶ Ideal conditions

**Water:** Slightly acidic, slightly soft.
**Temperature:** 18-23°C (64-73°F).
**Food:** Small live or frozen aquatic invertebrates, such as daphnia, mosquito larvae and bloodworm. Flake foods. Green foods.
**Minimum number in the aquarium:** 2.
**Minimum tank size:** 60cm (24in).
**Tank region:** Bottom, middle and top.

**Left:** *Pairs of fish will break away from the shoal and spawn in the community aquarium – where the other inmates usually consider the eggs a free meal!*

### ▶ Breeding

Rosy barbs breed by scattering their eggs over fine-leaved plants. They can produce several hundred eggs but the parents will eat them, so remove the adults after spawning. It takes about 30 hours for the eggs to hatch and the fry will feed greedily on fine foods.

# GOLDEN DWARF BARB ● *Barbus gelius*

FAMILY: CYPRINIDAE (BARBS)

You may see this fish described as the gelius barb or the golden barb (but do not confuse it with the much larger *Barbus schuberti,* which is also sold as the golden barb!). These small fish are a useful addition to an aquarium that has been up and running for four to six months. Be sure to keep them in a shoal, as they feel unsafe unless they are in a larger group. Single – or even three or four – specimens tend to sulk away in dark areas of the aquarium. Give them room to swim, as well as shady areas to retire to.

These barbs will live quite happily with other small species and are no problem to feed, providing the foods are small enough to fit into their mouths. This is important, otherwise they will starve. They also graze on soft algae and pick at peas and lettuce.

## Ideal conditions

**Water:** Slightly acidic, soft.
**Temperature:** 18-23°C (64-73°F).
**Food:** Tiny live or frozen aquatic invertebrates, such as daphnia, mosquito larvae and bloodworm. Very small flake and green foods.
**Minimum number in the aquarium:** 6.
**Minimum tank size:** 45cm (18in).
**Tank region:** Middle.

*Distinguishing the sexes can be difficult with golden dwarf barbs, but in healthy specimens, the males are generally slimmer than the females and have a deeper, almost copper-coloured stripe along their sides.*

## Origins

*Slow-flowing streams, rivers and pools in India, Bengal and Assam.*

*Feeding small live or frozen foods brings out the best colours on this little barb.*

## Breeding

The fish lay their eggs on the undersides of leaves and a single pair may produce up to 100 eggs. Like many barbs, the parents will eat the spawn. The fry hatch out after 24 hours and require very tiny first foods.

FAMILY: CYPRINIDAE (BARBS)

The ruby barb's common name can be misleading, because it is only the male that exhibits the rich red colour. The fish are also known as black ruby barbs and purple-headed barbs, so clearly the colours can vary! The colours are at their best when the males are ready to breed, so keep a group of both sexes.

You can keep these active little shoaling fish in a mixed shoal with other small barbs that have vertical stripes. They have no bad habits, other than occasionally nibbling at the plants, and will not harass other fish. Provide plenty of open water for them to swim in and use some broad-leaved plants to create sheltered, dimly lit areas for them to retire to.

### Breeding

Ruby barbs are egg-scatterers and the parents may eat their spawn, so remove them after spawning. The eggs hatch in 24 hours and the fry take small live foods.

### Conditioning

*These fish benefit from a cooler spell during the winter months, when the tank temperature can be reduced to 20-22°C (68-72°F). This keeps them in good shape, especially for breeding. Return the temperature to the higher end of the range in summer. Do check that any other species in your aquarium can cope with this before you do it. The ruby barbs will not suffer if they are kept at a constant temperature, but they may not breed.*

### Origins

*Sluggish mountain streams in Sri Lanka.*

### Ideal conditions

**Water:** Slightly acidic to neutral, soft to slightly hard.
**Temperature:** 20-26°C (68-79°F).
**Food:** Small live or frozen aquatic invertebrates, such as daphnia, mosquito larvae and bloodworm. Flake foods. A supply of green foods, such as peas and lettuce, deters the fish from eating plants.
**Minimum number in the aquarium:** 4.
**Minimum tank size:** 60cm (24in).
**Tank region:** Bottom, middle and top.

# CHEQUER BARB ● *Barbus oligolepis*

FAMILY: CYPRINIDAE (BARBS)

This little barb is useful for novice fishkeepers because it is easy to keep. Be sure to buy at least six of them because they really do like to be kept this way. It also ensures that you have both sexes. Males will sometimes spar with each other but very rarely do each other any damage. They are merely establishing their place within the shoal, as well as trying to entice willing females to spawn. Their sparring is not usually aimed at other tankmates. They like swimming space, so keep all plants to the sides and rear of the aquarium. They will eat just about anything they can get into their mouths and given a varied diet, these fish grow fast and can be sexually mature in less than six months.

## Coloration

*To see the iridescent sheen on the body, you must offer the fish some green foods, such as soft algae or lettuce and peas. A weekly feed of live or frozen foods is also beneficial, especially if you are intending to breed the fish.*

## Origins

*Streams and rivers in most of Indonesia.*

*As the fish mature, the males develop more intense coloration and dark edges to their fins.*

## Ideal conditions

**Water:** Slightly acidic, slightly soft.
**Temperature:** 18-23°C (64-73°F).
**Food:** Small live or frozen aquatic invertebrates, such as daphnia, mosquito larvae and bloodworm. Flake foods. Green foods.
**Minimum number in the aquarium:** 6.
**Minimum tank size:** 60cm (24in).
**Tank region:** Bottom and middle.

# FIVE-BANDED BARB ● *Barbus pentazona*

FAMILY: CYPRINIDAE (BARBS)

Five-banded barbs have not always been considered suitable fish for beginners. However, the fish imported today are often tank-raised and well acclimatised to aquarium conditions, so fishkeepers with a little experience could add them to their aquariums. You can overcome their natural timidity by keeping them in a well-planted aquarium that will provide cover should they feel threatened.

Like the majority of barbs, they prefer the company of their own kind, but they may also be combined with other peaceful species. As long as you keep them at the upper end of their temperature range and are able to provide a varied diet of live and/or frozen foods you should not have any problems. They are notorious for refusing to take flakes, but with tank-raised stock, this is proving to be less of a problem. They are difficult to breed and the fry are hard to raise.

*Males and females look very similar but they can be distinguished when they reach maturity. The males are slimmer and more brightly coloured than the females.*

### ▶ Origins

Southeast Asia: Malay Peninsula, Singapore and Borneo.

## ▶ Ideal conditions

**Water:** Slightly acidic to neutral, soft to slightly hard.
**Temperature:** 22-26°C (72-79°F).
**Food:** Small live or frozen aquatic invertebrates, such as daphnia, mosquito larvae and bloodworm. Flake foods. Green foods.
**Minimum number in the aquarium:** 4.
**Minimum tank size:** 60cm (24in).
**Tank region:** Middle.

FAMILY: CYPRINIDAE (BARBS)

The tiger barb has a well-deserved reputation as a bully and a fin-nipper. However, by understanding the needs of these highly attractive fish, it is possible to keep them without the usual chaos in the aquarium.

House them in large groups of at least eight specimens. They like to establish a pecking order within the shoal and, apart from the odd rogue fish, will normally be happily occupied maintaining this pecking order rather than nipping and harassing other tankmates. Choose these tankmates with utmost care. Avoid species that are slow-moving or have long trailing fins, such as guppies, angelfish, Siamese fighters and gouramis.

Several variable colour forms are available: albino, red and green, but all retain the same nasty habits!

## Ideal conditions

**Water:** Slightly acidic to neutral, soft to slightly hard.
**Temperature:** 20-26°C (68-79°F).
**Food:** Small live or frozen aquatic invertebrates, such as daphnia, mosquito larvae and bloodworm. Flake foods. Green foods.
**Minimum number in the aquarium:** 8.
**Minimum tank size:** 60cm (24in).
**Tank region:** Middle.

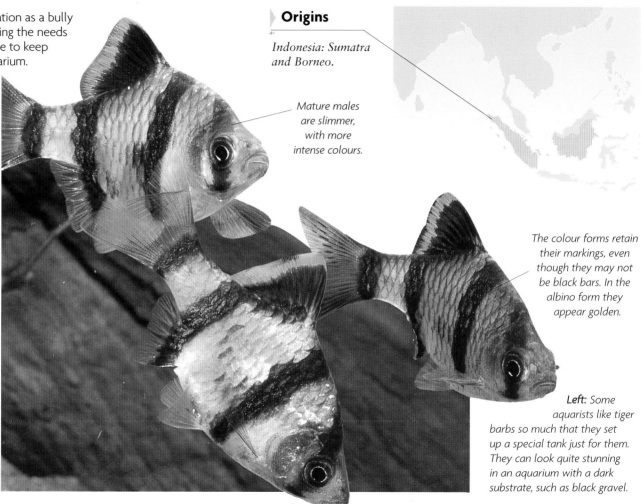

## Origins

*Indonesia: Sumatra and Borneo.*

*Mature males are slimmer, with more intense colours.*

*The colour forms retain their markings, even though they may not be black bars. In the albino form they appear golden.*

*Left: Some aquarists like tiger barbs so much that they set up a special tank just for them. They can look quite stunning in an aquarium with a dark substrate, such as black gravel.*

# TWO-SPOT BARB or TICTO BARB ● *Barbus ticto*

FAMILY: CYPRINIDAE (BARBS)

Two-spot barbs are often overlooked in dealers' tanks because they do not show their best colours until they are mature, and even then it can be difficult to tell males from females outside the breeding season. (Females do not usually have spots on their dorsal fins. Mature males are slimmer, have black spots on the edge of the dorsal fin and a reddish band along the body.) However, it is well worth trying to keep these creatures, as they are probably one of the best small barbs for the community aquarium. They will quickly settle in a shoal with other small species, provided there is enough open water for them to do so.

Feed them plenty of frozen foods, such as bloodworm, or small live foods if you can get them, as well as flakes. A varied diet will help to produce healthy fish with good colour.

*Like any active fish, barbs can easily dislodge scales if they catch on sharp objects in the aquarium.*

## ► Origins

*Rivers and streams in India and Sri Lanka to the Himalayas.*

## ► Ideal conditions

**Water:** Slightly acidic to neutral, soft to slightly hard.
**Temperature:** 18-23°C (64-73°F).
**Food:** Small live or frozen aquatic invertebrates, such as daphnia, mosquito larvae and bloodworm. Flake foods. Green foods.
**Minimum number in the aquarium:** 4.
**Minimum tank size:** 60cm (24in).
**Tank region:** Bottom, middle and top.

## ► Breeding

The fish breed in warmer water, with one male spawning with several females. The eggs are scattered over plants and hatch in 24 to 36 hours. The fry will take tiny foods.

# CHERRY BARB • *Barbus titteya*

Family: Cyprinidae (Barbs)

Cherry barbs are gregarious and popular little fish that get their common name from the deep red colour of the males. By contrast, the female is pale brown with a darker brown stripe that runs from the snout through the eye, along the body to the caudal peduncle. Bred by the thousand for the aquarium trade, the fish are now under threat in the wild.

Cherry barbs are very peaceful. They gather together in a shoal and then go their separate ways to rest quietly among the plants on their own. This is quite normal behaviour. Young fish show little of the adult colours, but given plenty of frozen and live foods, supplemented with flakes and some green foods, they grow quickly.

*Below:* Cherry barbs quickly settle to life in the community aquarium and can grow quite rapidly if well fed.

## Origins

*Shady streams and rivers in the lowlands of Sri Lanka.*

## Ideal conditions

**Water:** Slightly acidic to neutral, soft to slightly hard.
**Temperature:** 23-26°C (73-79°F).
**Food:** Small live or frozen aquatic invertebrates, such as daphnia, mosquito larvae and bloodworm. Flake foods. Green foods.
**Minimum number in the aquarium:** 4.
**Minimum tank size:** 45cm (18in).
**Tank region:** Bottom, middle and top.

## Breeding

When breeding, the pair pass over fine-leaved plants, depositing one to three eggs at each pass. You can see the eggs quite clearly, attached to the plants by a fine thread. The fish carry on in this manner until they have laid as many as 300 eggs. However, do beware; the parents will eat their eggs! With any luck you will see tiny fry hatching after 24 hours and they will take fine live foods.

# PEARL DANIO ● *Brachydanio albolineatus*

FAMILY: CYPRINIDAE (DANIOS)

In the aquarium, these very active small fishes prefer a long tank where they can swim against a gentle current of water. Plant the aquarium along the back and sides, being sure to leave the main area open for the fish to swim. They are peaceful and may be kept with other similar-sized, placid species, such as some of the rasboras, other danios and some of the smaller barbs. They are undemanding provided you remember to do regular water changes. Should you forget and the water quality drops, they may become sluggish and hide away or even refuse to feed. Normally, pearl danios greedily accept offerings of flakes, live, frozen and freeze-dried foods; a mixed diet helps them retain their subtle coloration. A yellow form of this fish is sometimes available.

## Breeding

All danios breed by scattering their eggs over plants. In warm, fresh water only 10-15cm (4-6in) deep, a trio of fish (two males and one female) will spawn over fine-leaved plants. Move the parents after spawning because they will eat the eggs. The eggs can take up to 48 hours to hatch and the fry need tiny live foods.

## Origins

*Streams and rivers in Southeast Asia: Burma, Thailand, the Malay Peninsula and Sumatra.*

The fine barbels can quickly deteriorate in poor conditions.

Females are deeper-bodied than the males.

## Ideal conditions

**Water:** Slightly acidic to neutral, soft to slightly hard.
**Temperature:** 20-25°C (68-77°F).
**Food:** Small live or frozen aquatic invertebrates, such as daphnia, mosquito larvae and bloodworm. Flake foods. Green foods.
**Minimum number in the aquarium:** 4.
**Minimum tank size:** 60cm (24in).
**Tank region:** Middle to top.

# ZEBRA DANIO ● *Brachydanio rerio*

FAMILY: CYPRINIDAE (DANIOS)

When you see the deep blue and gold stripes along the body of mature healthy specimens, you will agree that the common name zebra danio is an obvious choice for these highly popular aquarium fish. (An albino form and a long-finned variety are also available.) A shoal is constantly on the move around the tank but causes no problems, blending well with other species of similar temperament. It is not easy to distinguish the sexes in young stock, but mature males have more intense coloration and are slimmer than females. In a group of four fish you should end up with at least one pair, but to increase the chances, buy six.

Allow the fish plenty of swimming space. Thickets of plants will provide hiding places should the fish need them.

## Breeding

Zebra danios are easy to breed, provided the fish are allowed to pair themselves from the shoal and are well fed on live foods to bring them into breeding condition. A full-grown pair will scatter anything up to 500 eggs over plants. These hatch in about 48 hours; the fry will eat commercial fry foods, as well as tiny live foods.

## Origins

*Eastern India, from Calcutta to Masulipatam.*

*In good quality fish, the lines along the flanks are unbroken.*

## Ideal conditions

**Water:** Slightly acidic to neutral, soft to slightly hard.
**Temperature:** 18-24°C (64-75°F).
**Food:** Small live or frozen aquatic invertebrates, such as daphnia, mosquito larvae and bloodworm. Flake foods. Green foods and algae.
**Minimum number in the aquarium:** 4.
**Minimum tank size:** 60cm (24in).
**Tank region:** Middle to top.

# GIANT DANIO ● *Danio aequipinnatus*

**Size:** *Males and females 10cm (4in)*

FAMILY: CYPRINIDAE (DANIOS)

The giant danio is always on the move, so much so that it could be described as restless. It is quite tolerant of other fish, but never keep it with anything that may harass or intimidate it. Some of the larger rainbowfish, for example, would compete for the same swimming space. Keep any planting to the rear and sides of the tank and allow one or two broadleaved plants to reach the surface so that the fish can retire between the leaves. Such cover also helps deter the fish from jumping out of the aquarium.

### Safety first

*The giant danio requires space and a quiet aquarium, as it is easily frightened and will readily jump to avoid potential danger. Use a cover glass!*

### Ideal conditions

**Water:** Slightly acidic to neutral, soft to slightly hard.
**Temperature:** 22-24°C (72-75°F).
**Food:** Small live or frozen aquatic invertebrates, such as daphnia, mosquito larvae and bloodworm. Flake foods. Green foods. Be sure to offer a varied diet.
**Minimum number in the aquarium:** 4.
**Minimum tank size:** 75cm (30in).
**Tank region:** Middle to top.

### Breeding

Males are slimmer than females. Giant danios lay their eggs on plants over a period of time; each time the pair come together about 8-10 eggs are laid and this process continues until the female is spent. By this time, a full-grown pair may have produced as many as 300 eggs. Move the parents after spawning and the eggs will hatch in around 36 hours. Feed the fry on small live foods.

### Origins

*Streams and pools on the west coast of India and Sri Lanka.*

*The colour and markings on these fish can vary depending on the quality of the breeding stock – something over which we have little control.*

# WHITE CLOUD MOUNTAIN MINNOW • *Tanichthys albonubes*

**Size:** *Males and females 4cm (1.6in)*

FAMILY: CYPRINIDAE (WHITE CLOUD MOUNTAIN MINNOWS)

This colourful little fish is often overlooked because of its small size, but if you only have room for a small tank it should be top of your list. The main thing to remember is that white clouds cannot stand too much warmth for a protracted period of time.

White clouds like a tank with thickets of plants for shelter and the company of their own kind, so be sure to keep them in a shoal of at least six. If these conditions are not met, the fish will become very timid and sulk in the corner of the tank, while their beautiful colours will pale into insignificance.

**Other forms**

*A long-finned variety is also available. It is more trouble to keep as it requires slightly warmer conditions, otherwise it may suffer from bacterial infections.*

## ▶ Origins

*Streams on the White Cloud Mountain, near Canton, southern China.*

*Males are more colourful, slim fish, while the females are more rounded.*

## ▶ Breeding

The male courts his chosen female, spreading his fins and swimming round her until the pair come together and swim over some fine-leaved plants, shedding spawn and milt (sperm). The eggs hatch after 36 hours and the fry need fine live foods. These fish are so easy to breed in cool conditions that many aquarists put them outside during the warm summer months and the fish breed readily in plant-filled ponds and tubs.

***Left:** Even in the community aquarium, white cloud mountain minnows will come into spawning condition. If you are lucky, you can watch the males court and spawn with the well-rounded females.*

## ▶ Ideal conditions

**Water:** Neutral, soft to slightly hard.
**Temperature:** 18-23°C (64-73°F).
**Food:** Small live or frozen aquatic invertebrates, such as daphnia, mosquito larvae and bloodworm. Flake foods. Offer a varied diet.
**Minimum number in the aquarium:** 6.
**Minimum tank size:** 45cm (18in).
**Tank region:** Middle to top.

# RED-TAILED RASBORA • *Rasbora borapetensis*

FAMILY: CYPRINIDAE (RASBORAS)

Provided you have arranged your aquarium decor so that there is some open water, these small shoaling fish like being kept with other small shoaling species, such as the zebra danio. With plants around the sides and back and low-growing plants towards the front, the red-tailed rasboras will be happy, darting out of the security of the plants to swim around with the other fish. Red-tailed rasboras are not easy to sex, especially as youngsters, but because you will be buying a group of them, there is every chance that it will contain at least one fish of each sex. As the fish grow up, males will become recognisable as slimmer than the deep-bodied females.

*Maintaining good water quality helps to keep these fish in good health.*

## Origins

Southeast Asia: Thailand and the Malay Peninsula.

*Include some frozen daphnia and bloodworm in the diet to maintain the beautiful iridescent sheen on the body. The fish also relish live foods, such as mosquito larvae.*

## Ideal conditions

**Water:** Slightly acidic to neutral, soft to slightly hard.
**Temperature:** 22-26°C (72-79°F).
**Food:** Small live or frozen aquatic invertebrates, such as daphnia, mosquito larvae and bloodworm. Flake foods.
**Minimum number in the aquarium:** 4.
**Minimum tank size:** 45cm (18in).
**Tank region:** Middle to top.

# HARLEQUIN ● *Rasbora heteromorpha*

FAMILY: CYPRINIDAE (RASBORAS)

In a tank with planted areas and some open water, harlequins will have room to swim as well as quieter, dimly lit areas beneath the plants to which they can retire. Harlequins like the company of their own kind, but will also shoal with other rasboras and danios. Most beginners want to add this very popular aquarium fish to the tank straightaway, but patience is the key. Make sure that your tank has settled down and that you have started to master water changes, filter cleaning, feeding, etc. Wait six to nine months before you try keeping these fish, otherwise they will quickly perish. On a varied diet that includes small frozen and even live foods, the fish will be more robust and have much better colour. Regular water changes are essential to keep them healthy.

*In females there is a straight leading edge to the dark marking on the side. In males the bottom of the mark is slightly rounded and the tip is extended.*

**Above:** *Harlequins breed in a strange manner. They invert in order to lay their eggs on the underside of broad leaves.*

## ▶ Origins

*Southeast Asia: Thailand, Malaysia, Singapore and some areas in Sumatra.*

## ▶ Ideal conditions

**Water:** Slightly acidic to neutral, soft to slightly hard.
**Temperature:** 22-25°C (72-77°F).
**Food:** Small live or frozen aquatic invertebrates, such as daphnia, mosquito larvae and bloodworm. Flake foods.
**Minimum number in the aquarium:** 8.
**Minimum tank size:** 45cm (18in).
**Tank region:** Middle to top.

# RED-LINE RASBORA ● *Rasbora pauciperforata*

FAMILY: CYPRINIDAE (RASBORAS)

Often overlooked in dealers' tanks because of its lack of colour, this lively little rasbora quickly settles into an aquarium and, if fed a wide variety of foods, soon develops a bold red line along its flanks. These peaceful shoaling fish feel safe in a group of at least four and happily coexist with other midwater-swimming fishes of a similar size.

Regular water changes are essential, otherwise these fish will suffer. If you notice them sulking away in a corner or just lurking in the plants, their colour faded and their fins clamped, this is a sure sign that there is a potential problem. Take prompt action; something as simple as a water change will usually correct the conditions and the fish will soon be out and about again.

## ▶ Breeding

Males are generally slimmer than females. These egglayers are notoriously difficult to breed because they are selective about their partners. If you do have a compatible pair, they will lay their eggs among fine-leaved plants. Hatching takes about 24 hours and the fry require very small foods.

## ▶ Origins

*Southeast Asia: western Malaysia and Sumatra.*

*The fins of this fish can sometimes appear translucent yellow. This is perfectly normal.*

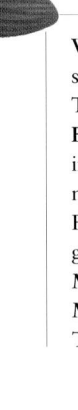

*These fish relish small live foods.*

## ▶ Ideal conditions

**Water:** Slightly acidic to neutral, soft to slightly hard.
**Temperature:** 23-25°C (73-77°F).
**Food:** Live or frozen small aquatic invertebrates, such as daphnia, mosquito larvae and bloodworm. Flake foods. The fish also enjoy grazing on soft algae and lettuce.
**Minimum number in the aquarium:** 4
**Minimum tank size:** 60cm (24in).
**Tank region:** Middle to top.

# SCISSORTAIL or THREE-LINED RASBORA • *Rasbora trilineata*

FAMILY: CYPRINIDAE (RASBORAS)

Scissortails are among the larger rasboras, so keep them in a long aquarium with plenty of swimming space. Position plants to the back and sides to provide cover should they be scared; this will help to curb their desire to jump out of danger! They like a tank with a gentle current of water to swim against. Regular water changes are essential.

These fish are no trouble at all to feed. They take flake foods from the surface and such is their eagerness to feed that they will sometimes flip out of the water. Remember, that a varied diet makes for a healthier fish, so do offer alternative foods, such as frozen bloodworm and live foods.

Scissortails can be susceptible to white spot if conditions are not quite right, if there is a sudden change of temperature or if they are stressed by inappropriate tankmates. Do not keep them with larger fish that may harass them.

**Safety first**

*These lively, active fish tend to jump when frightened, so do not forget to put a cover glass on the tank.*

## Origins

*The lakes, rivers and streams of western Malaysia, Sumatra and Borneo.*

*These fish can easily damage their bodies when jumping.*

## Ideal conditions

**Water:** Slightly acidic to neutral, soft to slightly hard.
**Temperature:** 23-25°C (73-77°F).
**Food:** Small live or frozen aquatic invertebrates, such as daphnia, mosquito larvae and bloodworm. Flake foods.
**Minimum number in the aquarium:** 4.
**Minimum tank size:** 60cm (24in).
**Tank region:** Middle to top.

# FLYING FOX ● *Epalzeorhynchus kalopterus*

FAMILY: CYPRINIDAE (FLYING FOXES)

Once your aquarium has settled down, the flying fox is a useful fish for picking away at algae, but it will not eat thread algae; you will have to get rid of that yourself! It will also eat planarian worms, which makes it a useful biological control, preferable to treating the aquarium with chemicals to get rid of these pests. However, these eating habits do not mean that you need not feed the fish; they will take flake, tablet and granular foods, but relish live and green foods.

Flying foxes can be territorial, so keep just one in a 60cm (24in) tank, otherwise they will pick on each other, which could result in the death of the weaker fish. This aside, they are quite endearing characters that spend a lot of time resting on their pectoral fins on leaves or rocks. In a planted aquarium with well-oxygenated water, you will often see them 'playing' in the outflow from the filter system. Regular water changes and efficient filtration are essential to keep them healthy.

## ▶ Ideal conditions

**Water:** Slightly acidic to neutral, soft to slightly hard.
**Temperature:** 24-26°C (75-79°F).
**Food:** Small live or frozen aquatic invertebrates, such as daphnia, mosquito larvae and bloodworm. Flake foods. Green foods.
**Maximum number in a 60cm (24in) aquarium:** 1. More in a larger tank.
**Minimum tank size:** 60cm (24in).
**Tank region:** Bottom to middle.

### Other species

Crossocheilus siamensis, *the Siamese flying fox, is a little less colourful than* E. kalopterus, *but a useful addition to the aquarium, especially as it does eat thread algae! It is generally considered to be one of the best algae eaters available. Neither fish has been bred in captivity.*

## ▶ Origins

*Northern India, Burma, western Thailand, the Malay Peninsula, Sumatra and Borneo.*

*Maintain the colours on the fish by feeding it a varied diet.*

*Rapid breathing can sometimes be a sign that the oxygen levels are dropping. Check your filtration system.*

# AFRICAN RED-EYED CHARACIN ● *Arnoldichthys spilopterus*

FAMILY: ALESTIDAE (CHARACINS)

This peaceful, active characin is well-suited to a medium-sized planted aquarium. It will be quite happy alongside other similarly-sized, peaceful fishes with which it can shoal. Provide swimming space, plus planted areas where the light levels are reduced so that the red-eyed characin can seek refuge if frightened. Although this fish flourishes in a mature tank with good-quality water, it is not too fond of major water changes. It is far better to carry out regular, two-weekly water changes of, say, 10%, than three or four weekly changes of 15-20%. In a dealer's tank, the fish often lack the iridescent sheen on the body because the tank is not to their liking, but in a suitably planted aquarium and with careful feeding that includes plenty of live foods, the fish will soon show their delicate colours to best advantage.

## Ideal conditions

**Water:** Slightly acidic to neutral, soft to slightly hard.
**Temperature:** 22-28°C (72-83°F).
**Food:** Small live or frozen aquatic invertebrates, such as daphnia, mosquito larvae and bloodworm. Flake foods.
**Minimum number in the aquarium:** 2.
**Minimum tank size:** 90cm (36in).
**Tank region:** Middle.

## Origins

*Tropical West Africa: Lagos to the Niger Delta.*

## Breeding

A single pair can produce over 1,000 eggs, which hatch in 30-36 hours. The fry become free-swimming a week later. They are easy to feed and will grow rapidly on a first diet of fine foods and then on small live foods.

*The slim-bodied males sometimes appear underfed even when they are not!*

*The fish are quite easy to sex, as the male's anal fin is convex and coloured with red, yellow and black stripes, while the female has a straight-edged anal fin that is clear with a black point.*

# CONGO TETRA ● *Phenacogrammus interruptus*

FAMILY: CHARACIDAE (CHARACINS)

The Congo Tetra is one of the most impressive medium-sized characins. The fish love to swim, so allow for this by careful planting that gives them plenty of open water to move about in. They are susceptible to disease if water conditions deteriorate, so do not forget the water changes! Feeding is simple; they will eat dried foods but, to maintain the body sheen, be sure to include live foods or their frozen equivalents. Congos can be nervous, especially if you try keeping them in small numbers; they need the security of the shoal. Avoid keeping them with fish that are likely to nibble their finnage.

## Compatibility

*Male Congo tetras can be quarrelsome with each other, so do not try to crowd them.*

## Origins

*The Zaire River and nearby lakes in Central Africa.*

## Ideal conditions

**Water:** Slightly acidic to neutral, slightly soft.
**Temperature:** 22-26°C (72-79°F).
**Food:** Small live or frozen aquatic invertebrates, such as daphnia, mosquito larvae and bloodworm. Flake foods.
**Minimum number in the aquarium:** 6.
**Minimum tank size:** 90cm (36in).
**Tank region:** Middle.

*The clearly visible scales and intense coloration add to the charm of these creatures.*

*Mature males are easy to distinguish by their extended finnage and ragged-looking caudal fin.*

## Breeding

Congo tetras often spawn in the tank, scattering their large eggs over fine-leaved plants. Set up in a breeding tank, a pair can be triggered by a water change or early morning sunlight. Eggs hatch in six days; feed the fry newly hatched brineshrimp.

# BLOODFIN • *Aphyocharax anisitsi*

FAMILY: CHARACIDAE (CHARACINS)

The bloodfin is one of the easiest characins for the novice to keep. This small schooling fish makes few demands with regard to water quality or even temperature. It is a long-lived species; a ten-year life span is not unreasonable if the fish is well looked after. Like the White Cloud Mountain minnow, it can be kept in cool conditions, but shows much better colour if the water is slightly warm; 22-23°C (72-73°F) is ideal. Leave room among the plants so that the fish can swim about together as they would in the wild. Keep them with other small, peaceful species.

## Breeding

The fish breed by scattering their eggs among fine-leaved plants. Anything up to 500 eggs can result from a successful spawning, but the adults are quick to eat their own spawn, so remove them. The fry are reasonably easy to raise on crumbled flake and tiny live foods.

## Origins

*Argentina: in the Parana River.*

*Males have a slightly hooked anal fin and a slimmer body.*

## Ideal conditions

**Water:** Slightly acidic to neutral, soft to slightly hard.
**Temperature:** 18-28°C (64-82°F).
**Food:** Eagerly consumes small live or frozen aquatic invertebrates, such as daphnia, mosquito larvae and bloodworm. Flake foods.
**Minimum number in the aquarium:** 4, but 6 in a planted tank is better.
**Minimum tank size:** 60cm (24in).
**Tank region:** Middle.

# SILVER-TIPPED TETRA ● *Hasemania nana*

FAMILY: CHARACIDAE (CHARACINS)

The silver-tipped tetra, so-called because of the light tips to its fins, is well-suited to a community aquarium of peaceful fishes. In typical tetra fashion, it shoals in vast numbers in patches of open water and seeks refuge among plants when danger threatens. In the wild, it inhabits small streams with a good flow of highly oxygenated water. Accordingly, you should plant the aquarium with thickets of plants and leave some open areas. Ensure that the filtration system is working efficiently and providing well-oxygenated water. Being quite robust, it is one of the first characins that you can add to a community tank about a month after you have added your first fish.

## Ideal conditions

**Water:** Slightly acidic to neutral, soft to slightly hard.
**Temperature:** 22-28°C (72-82°F).
**Food:** Small live or frozen aquatic invertebrates, such as daphnia, mosquito larvae and bloodworm. Flake foods. Provide a varied diet.
**Minimum number in the aquarium:** 4.
**Minimum tank size:** 60cm (24in).
**Tank region:** Middle.

## Origins

*Eastern Brazil, River Sao Francisco basin; western Brazil, in the tributaries of the River Purus.*

*Mature males appear slimmer than females and have a white tip to the anal fin, whereas the female's anal fin has a yellowish tip.*

## Breeding

These little egglayers will produce about 300 eggs but take care – the parents will eat the eggs. For first foods, offer newly hatched brineshrimp and, as the fish grow, increase the size of the live foods.

# GLOWLIGHT ● *Hemigrammus erythrozonus*

**Size:** *Males and females 4cm (1.6in)*

FAMILY: CHARACIDAE (CHARACINS)

Glowlights are bred by the thousand on fish farms, just for the tropical fish industry. The majority of fish we buy now are raised in this way and have been acclimatised to suit the conditions found in the average community aquarium. They are, therefore, an excellent choice for the novice. Buy a small shoal, feed them well and they will reward you with good colour and plenty of activity. The origin of the common name is obvious – the bright red line that runs the length of the fish.

Although glowlights will accept all the usual small aquarium foods, you do need to pay some attention to the feeding regime. The fish prefer to be fed small amounts two or three times a day, rather than a single meal in the morning or evening, although they will survive on this. The little-and-often feeding regime really comes into play if you wish to bring them into breeding condition.

## Breeding

Males are slimmer than females. Breeding is typical of the tetras, with the eggs being scattered over plants. Feed the fry regular small feeds of tiny live foods.

## Ideal conditions

**Water:** Slightly acidic to neutral, soft to slightly hard.
**Temperature:** 23-28°C (73-82°F).
**Food:** Small live or frozen aquatic invertebrates, such as daphnia, mosquito larvae and bloodworm. Flake foods.
**Minimum number in the aquarium:** 4.
**Minimum tank size:** 60cm (24in).
**Tank region:** Middle.

## Origins

*Guyana: in the Essequibo River.*

*Contented fish display their colour and finnage to full advantage.*

*Carefully check the fish you buy. Due to inbreeding, they can sometimes exhibit deformities, unlike this good-looking fish.*

33

FAMILY: CHARACIDAE (CHARACINS)

You can almost see right through the body wall of this small characin. In fact, this helps you to distinguish the sexes, because in males the silvery swimbladder appears more pointed, while in females it is more rounded. The head and tail light is a good addition to the community aquarium, peaceful both with its own kind and with other fish. It spends much of its time among plants where it feels safe, but drop in the food and it is one of the first to get to it. Live foods bring out the best colours. If these are not available, offer the fish a good varied diet of frozen and flake foods.

Be sure to carry out regular water changes and check that the filtration system is working efficiently, as the fish like well-oxygenated, clean water. The water changes will also help to prevent a build-up of nitrates, which the fish will not tolerate.

*The larger the shoal, the more willing the head and tail light is to venture out into the aquarium.*

### ▶ Breeding

An easy characin to breed. In soft, acidic, warm conditions the fish will scatter their eggs over fine-leaved plants. Raise the fry on newly hatched brineshrimp.

### ▶ **Origins**

*Widespread in South America, from French Guiana to Argentina.*

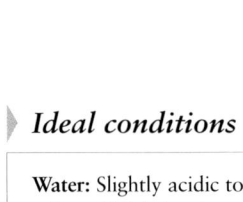

### ▶ *Ideal conditions*

**Water:** Slightly acidic to neutral, soft to slightly hard.
**Temperature:** 22-28°C (72-82°F).
**Food:** Small live or frozen aquatic invertebrates, such as daphnia, mosquito larvae and bloodworm. Flake foods.
**Minimum number in the aquarium:** 4.
**Minimum tank size:** 60cm (24in).
**Tank region:** Middle.

FAMILY: CHARACIDAE (CHARACINS)

This brightly coloured tetra is often overlooked because it fails to show its true colours in the shop tank. Very young specimens also lack the elongated dorsal and anal finnage seen in adult males. But try them. The delicate pinkish red body colour and the distinctive red 'heart' mark on the flanks make them worthwhile. The fish normally available are wild-caught and can be difficult to acclimatise, so check that they have been in the shop for a while and are feeding well. Take care over water quality and carry out regular water changes to avoid any build up of nitrates. Once established in the aquarium, they will feed readily on flake but benefit greatly from frozen and live foods in their diet.

### Compatibility

*The bleeding heart tetra prefers to be kept with other smaller, peaceful fishes. In the company of boisterous tank-mates it just hides among the plants. Unusually for a tetra, you can keep a large group of these fish or just a pair, provided the pair have other tetras to swim with.*

### ▸ Origins

*Amazon Basin in Peru and Brazil.*

*Take care not to include fin-nipping species with these tetras.*

*Females are easily distinguished by their lighter colour and shorter fins.*

### ▸ Ideal conditions

**Water:** Slightly acidic to neutral, soft to slightly hard.
**Temperature:** 22-28°C (72-82°F).
**Food:** Small live or frozen aquatic invertebrates, such as daphnia, mosquito larvae and bloodworm. Flake foods.
**Minimum number in the aquarium:** 2.
**Minimum tank size:** 60cm (24in).
**Tank region:** Middle.

# BLACK NEON ● *Hyphessobrycon herbertaxelrodi*

FAMILY: CHARACIDAE (CHARACINS)

The black neon is another little characin that is farmed to supply the hobby. Wild-caught fish are very demanding in terms of water conditions, but farmed fish are much more tolerant – so much so that they can easily be kept in a community aquarium. Do not add them as starter fish, but after a month to six weeks they will be able to live quite happily in your aquarium, provided you are keeping other peaceful species.

Black neons are typical shoaling fish, spending some time hanging in the water just flicking their fins every now and then before swimming off for a while and then retiring to the plants.

*The fish should show good colour and swim with their fins erect, as here. If not, check the water conditions and rectify them if necessary.*

## ▶ Origins

*The Mato Grosso region of Brazil, in the Taquari River.*

## ▶ *Ideal conditions*

**Water:** Slightly acidic to neutral, soft to slightly hard.
**Temperature:** 22-28°C (72-82°F).
**Food:** Small live or frozen aquatic invertebrates, such as daphnia, mosquito larvae and bloodworm. Flake foods. A varied diet is vital to bring the fish into breeding condition.
**Minimum number in the aquarium:** 4.
**Minimum tank size:** 60cm (24in).
**Tank region:** Middle.

## ▶ *Breeding*

Adult males are slimmer than the females. They breed in soft acid water, scattering their eggs over fine-leaved plants. The eggs hatch in about 36 hours; feed the fry tiny live foods such as newly hatched brineshrimp.

# BLACK PHANTOM TETRA ● *Megalamphodus megalopterus*

*Size:* Males and females 4.5cm (1.8in)

FAMILY: CHARACIDAE (CHARACINS)

This small, predominantly black characin will add a little contrast to your aquarium. Fortunately, it is also one of the easiest tetras to maintain in captivity. It does not look its best in a dealer's tank; it requires the security of a well-planted aquarium and good feeding to settle down and show its true colours.

In the wild it is found in shady streams, so provide a tank with some planting, some open areas and a gentle current of water flowing through it. Choose companion fish with care. They should be peaceful and not the type to nip another fish's fins. The black phantom's large fins can be just too much of a temptation to some fish.

## ▶ Breeding

Given a varied diet, the fish will come into breeding condition and it is not unusual to see pairs displaying in the community aquarium. They are egg-scatterers and can be bred in soft, acidic conditions with subdued lighting. Feed the fry tiny live foods.

## ▶ **Origins**

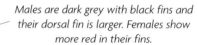

*In the River Sao Francisco, eastern Brazil.*

*Males are dark grey with black fins and their dorsal fin is larger. Females show more red in their fins.*

## ▶ *Ideal conditions*

**Water:** Slightly acidic to neutral, soft to slightly hard.
**Temperature:** 18-28°C (64-82°F).
**Food:** Small live or frozen aquatic invertebrates, such as daphnia, mosquito larvae and bloodworm. Flake foods.
**Minimum number in the aquarium:** 2.
**Minimum tank size:** 60cm (24in).
**Tank region:** Middle.

# DIAMOND TETRA ● *Moenkhausia pitteri*

FAMILY: CHARACIDAE (CHARACINS)

Diamond tetras will flourish in a peaceful, planted community aquarium. If possible, provide a gentle flow of water through the tank. A group of young fish, which are often overlooked in dealers' tanks because they have none of the flamboyant features of the adults, will quickly mature if fed a diet that incorporates plenty of small, live or frozen aquatic invertebrates. They accept flake food, but feeding the fish on this diet alone usually results in fish that lack the added sparkle.

### Ideal conditions

**Water:** Soft, slightly acidic.
**Temperature:** 24-28°C (75-82°F).
**Food:** Small live or frozen aquatic invertebrates, such as daphnia, mosquito larvae and bloodworm. Flake foods.
**Minimum number in the aquarium:** 6.
**Minimum tank size:** 60cm (24in).
**Tank region:** Middle.

### Origins

*Lake Valencia in northern Venezuela.*

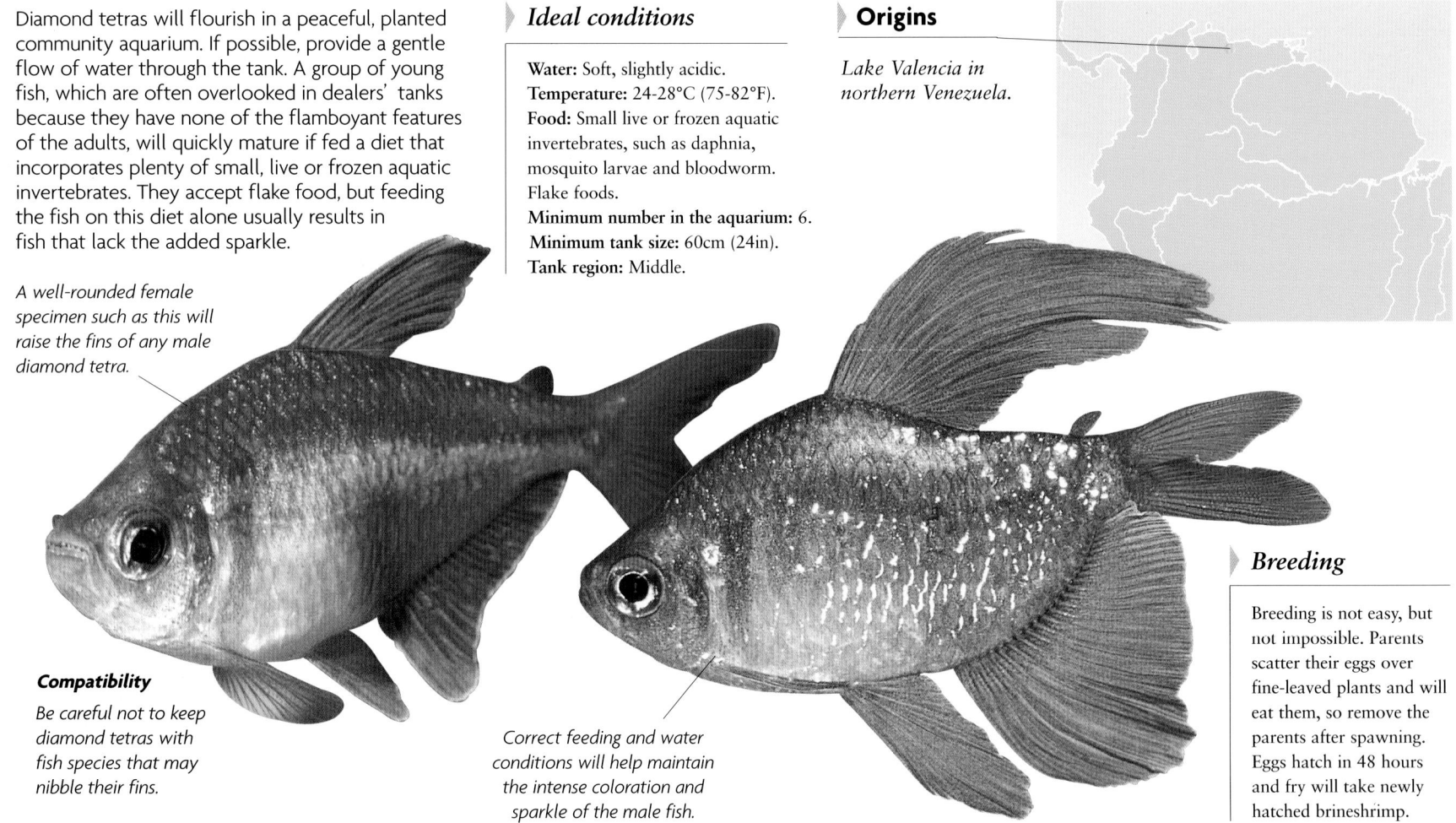

*A well-rounded female specimen such as this will raise the fins of any male diamond tetra.*

#### Compatibility

*Be careful not to keep diamond tetras with fish species that may nibble their fins.*

*Correct feeding and water conditions will help maintain the intense coloration and sparkle of the male fish.*

### Breeding

Breeding is not easy, but not impossible. Parents scatter their eggs over fine-leaved plants and will eat them, so remove the parents after spawning. Eggs hatch in 48 hours and fry will take newly hatched brineshrimp.

# CARDINAL TETRA • *Paracheirodon axelrodi*

FAMILY: CHARACIDAE (CHARACINS)

The brilliant colours of this characin make it one of the most popular aquarium fish, but it is not one of the easiest to keep. Do not introduce it into a newly set-up aquarium but wait until your system has settled down and see what the water parameters average out at. (This is one good reason for keeping an aquarium log!) You will need soft, slightly acidic conditions and a mature tank with well-established thickets of plants to provide shelter. Although they are expensive, it is well worth saving up to buy a shoal of these fish. Single fish tend to hide away, as do two or three, but they gain strength in numbers and will also look far more impressive. The vast majority of cardinals offered for sale are wild-caught and highly sought-after community fish.

## Breeding

Although the cardinal is an egg-layer and has been bred, it is not easy to do as they are extremely particular about water parameters. They can produce up to 500 eggs and the fry need very small live foods. It is worth noting that if kept in water that is too hard, fish and fry can suffer kidney damage.

## Origins

*Western Colombia and northeastern Brazil.*

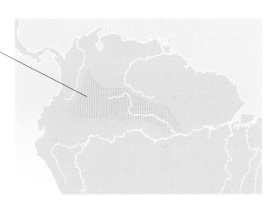

## Ideal conditions

**Water:** Slightly acidic, soft.
**Temperature:** 23-27°C (73-80°F).
**Food:** Tiny live or frozen aquatic invertebrates, such as daphnia, mosquito larvae and bloodworm that the fish can take with their small mouths. Flake foods.
**Minimum number in the aquarium:** 6.
**Minimum tank size:** 60cm (24in).
**Tank region:** Middle.

# NEON TETRA ● *Paracheirodon innesi*

FAMILY: CHARACIDAE (CHARACINS)

The neon tetra is probably the most popular of all aquarium fish. Today, nearly all the neons offered for sale are captive-bred and some shops offer a choice of size: youngsters at 1-1.5cm (0.4-0.6in) and 3-4cm (1.2-1.6in) adult fish. Neons are a long-lived species; a ten-year life span is not uncommon.

A planted tank with an open area in the middle will display the fish at their best. Some people keep a tank just for neons and use a dark substrate, such as black gravel, and plenty of plants to create a stunning display. Although these tank-raised fish will tolerate a wide range of water parameters, they will not tolerate poor water management, which results in low oxygen levels and high nitrate levels.

## Breeding

Breeding takes place in very soft acidic water and subdued lighting. The eggs are laid over fine-leaved plants and hatch in 24 hours. Feed the newly hatched fry on very fine live foods.

## Origins

*The River Putumayo in Peru.*

*Mature males are slimmer than females and have a straighter blue line along the flanks.*

### Safety first

*House this gentle little fish with like companions and, especially if you have bought small specimens, avoid keeping it with larger species, such as angels, because they will eat the small neons.*

## Ideal conditions

**Water:** Slightly acidic to neutral, soft to slightly hard.
**Temperature:** 20-26°C (68-79°F).
**Food:** Tiny live or frozen aquatic invertebrates, such as daphnia, mosquito larvae and bloodworm. Flake foods. Provide a varied diet to maintain the colours of the fish.
**Minimum number in the aquarium:** A shoal of at least 6 and preferably 10 fish, because they really are at their best when seen in numbers.
**Minimum tank size:** 60cm (24in).
**Tank region:** Middle.

# SPLASH TETRA • *Copella arnoldi*

**Size:** *Males 8cm (3.2in), females 6cm (2.4in)*

FAMILY: LEBIASINIDAE (CHARACINS)

These slightly larger characins for the community aquarium are active fish that like to be kept in shoals or at least pairs. It is difficult to distinguish between the sexes in young fish, so you would have to buy at least two! Keep them in an aquarium with a good cover glass, because they jump. They also like to feed from the surface and often flip from the water when doing so. A couple of floating plants will help deter jumping by giving the fish a secluded place to lurk in. Keep water conditions within bounds, ensuring that regular water changes and efficient filtration prevent any build up of nitrates.

These fish will eat just about anything from flies and flake floating on the surface to tablets that sink to the substrate. They also relish live or frozen food.

## Ideal conditions

**Water:** Slightly acidic to neutral, soft to slightly hard.
**Temperature:** 23-29°C (73-84°F).
**Food:** Small live or frozen aquatic invertebrates, such as daphnia, mosquito larvae and bloodworm. Flake foods.
**Minimum number in the aquarium:** 2.
**Minimum tank size:** 90cm (36in).
**Tank region:** Middle to top.

## Origins

*Guyana, lower Amazon.*

*Mature males are generally larger and more colourful than females and have more extended finnage.*

## Breeding

Splash, or jumping, tetras are so-called because of their method of spawning. To breed them, set up a special aquarium with a tight-fitting cover glass because, with their bodies pressed together, a pair will jump and lay their eggs on the underside of a leaf overhanging the water surface at the top of the tank. The pair then fall back into the water and repeat the process until some 150 eggs have been laid. The male guards the eggs, flicking water at them to keep them moist until they hatch and the fry fall into the water. Provide them with tiny live foods.

FAMILY: LEBIASINIDAE (CHARACINS)

Of all the pencilfish, this species is the easiest to keep. It will settle down well in a community aquarium with other small fishes, but can be intimidated by larger, more boisterous ones. Avoid extremes of pH and hardness and ensure that the filtration is working well, because the fish do not like water with a lot of suspended matter in it. Provide some sheltered areas in the form of thickets of fine-leaved plants.

Pencilfish can change their colour pattern. During the day you can see the prominent longitudinal stripes. At night or in very dim conditions, these stripes break up until only vertical bars are visible on the body. This is nothing to worry about; it is perfectly normal.

*Below: Having been well fed on plenty of live foods, this full-bodied female appears almost ready to spawn.*

### ▶ Origins

*Guyana and in the lower River Negro, in the central Amazon region of Brazil.*

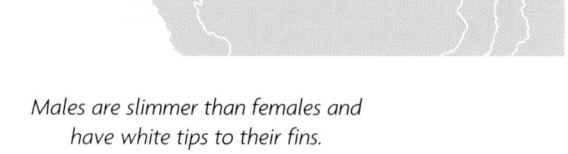

*Males are slimmer than females and have white tips to their fins.*

### ▶ *Ideal conditions*

**Water:** Slightly acidic to neutral, soft to slightly hard.
**Temperature:** 23-26°C (73-79°F).
**Food:** Tiny live or frozen aquatic invertebrates, such as daphnia, mosquito larvae and bloodworm that will fit into the fishes' small mouths. Regular feeds of live food maintain good coloration. Flake foods.
**Minimum number in the aquarium:** 2.
**Minimum tank size:** 60cm (24in).
**Tank region:** Middle.

# MOSQUITO FISH ● *Gambusia affinis*

FAMILY: POECILIIDAE (LIVEBEARERS)

This small livebearer is relatively trouble-free in an aquarium, provided you maintain good water conditions (which means do not forget the water changes and make sure the filter is working efficiently). You must also offer them a varied diet; they will not survive on flake alone.

Males are easily recognised by their smaller size, brighter coloration and gonopodium. Females are dull in comparison, with grey/silver bodies. In the wild, they are found in a wide range of habitats but are best kept towards the middle of their temperature and water ranges. Like the guppy, this fish has been used by man as a natural way to help control the spread of mosquitoes carrying malaria.

## Compatibility

*These are tough little fish that can be somewhat aggressive, so choose tankmates that can look after themselves. They may also pick on each other, so provide a planted tank in which they can avoid each other in the foliage.*

## Origins

*Florida to Texas and Mexico.*

*Below: Live foods, especially mosquito larvae, help to bring these fish into breeding condition. This is a male.*

## Ideal conditions

**Water:** Neutral, slightly hard.
**Temperature:** 20-28°C (68-83°F).
**Food:** Small live or frozen aquatic invertebrates, such as daphnia, mosquito larvae and bloodworm. Flake foods.
**Minimum number in the aquarium:** One pair.
**Minimum tank size:** 45cm (18in).
**Tank region:** Middle to top.

## Breeding

Mosquito fish are not easy to breed, so do not be surprised if you fail to see youngsters in your community aquarium. To induce breeding, pick an adult female and introduce several males. Then stabilise the water in the tank to 20-24°C (68-75°F) and add some floating plants to act as a refuge for the youngsters.

*Left: The generic name, Gambusia, is derived from the Cuban 'gambusino', meaning insignificant – hardly suitable for a fish that helps man by eating mosquito larvae. This is a female.*

FAMILY: POECILIIDAE (LIVEBEARERS)

This little livebearer is one of the smallest fish in the world and a good community fish in a densely planted aquarium with other fish of a similar size. Some aquarists like to devote a tank to this species alone. Mosquito fish will accept flake foods, but as their common name suggests, they eat mosquito larvae and will flourish if you can manage to feed some of these live or frozen. They also relish other small live or frozen foods, such as daphnia and brineshrimp. Remember, that these are tiny fish so you must offer them small foods that will fit into their mouths.

This fish is also sold under the names dwarf livebearer and dwarf top minnow.

## Ideal conditions

**Water:** Slightly acidic to slightly alkaline, slightly soft to slightly hard.
**Temperature:** 20-26°C (68-79°F)
**Food:** Small live or frozen aquatic invertebrates such as daphnia, mosquito larvae and bloodworm. Flake and green foods.
**Minimum number in the aquarium:** One pair.
**Minimum tank size:** 45cm (18in).
**Tank region:** Middle to top.

## Origins

*USA: South Carolina.*

*The colour of these fish, here a female, is greatly improved if their diet includes live foods.*

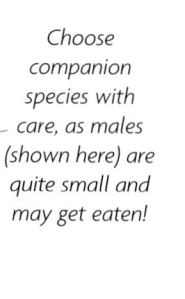

*Choose companion species with care, as males (shown here) are quite small and may get eaten!*

## Breeding

Sexing is easy because the males have a gonopodium and are much smaller than the females. The fish breed readily, with the female giving birth over a couple of weeks. In a well-planted tank housing mosquito fish only, many of the young will survive among the plants, but in a community aquarium quite a few will be devoured by other tankmates.

FAMILY: POECILIIDAE (LIVEBEARERS)

These magnificent fish are very popular but can be difficult to keep properly. They need the correct diet, sufficient space and only a gentle flow of water. They also require warmth and good-quality water; the hybrids in particular are susceptible to disease if conditions are not right. Wait until the aquarium has been established for six months or so to ensure stable conditions before you add these fish and then they should thrive.

The male uses his very large dorsal fin to display to females, and the anal fin is modified into a gonopodium. His light olive-coloured body looks silvery in bright light. Females are similarly coloured, but have a much smaller dorsal fin and no gonopodium. In some males, the dorsal fin may have a golden-orange edge and the same colour appears on the head and throat.

*Right: These fish have been developed to produce colour forms, such as marbled and black (as here). They also cross readily with other species. In the wild, naturally occurring crosses between Poecilia latipinna and P. mexicana have been recorded.*

## Breeding

The fish reach maturity in about nine months. A full-grown female may produce broods of up to 100 fry every month. The fry are large, up to 7mm (0.28in) in length when born. Given small live foods and plenty of algae to pick on, they grow rapidly.

## Origins

*Southeastern North Carolina to the Atlantic coast of Mexico.*

*The upturned mouth of the Molly is a clear indication that it feeds predominantly from the water surface.*

## Ideal conditions

**Water:** Neutral, hard.
**Temperature:** 25-28°C (77-82°F).
**Food:** Small live or frozen aquatic invertebrates, such as daphnia, mosquito larvae and bloodworm. Plenty of green foods. Flake foods.
**Minimum number in the aquarium:** One pair.
**Minimum tank size:** 90cm (36in).
**Tank region:** Middle to top.

# GUPPY or MILLIONS FISH • *Poecilia reticulata*

FAMILY: POECILIIDAE (LIVEBEARERS)

The guppy is one of the most popular aquarium fishes. It is bred commercially by the thousand and has been selectively bred to develop all the different colours and fin forms available today. These cultivated forms require higher temperatures than their wild counterparts. (Wild guppies are quite plain in comparison, but because they are rarely available, they are much sought after by dedicated hobbyists.) When buying your fish be sure to include males and females. The males are the favourites because of their long, flowing caudal fins and often gaudy colours. Although the females are less colourful – only their tails and sometimes the rear half of the body showing any colour – the males do require something to show off to. Guppies have been introduced in some tropical regions to control mosquitoes, as they love eating the larvae.

## Ideal conditions

**Water:** Neutral, hard.
**Temperature:** 18-28°C (64-82°F).
**Food:** Small live or frozen aquatic invertebrates, such as daphnia, mosquito larvae and bloodworm. Flake foods.
**Minimum number in the aquarium:** One pair.
**Minimum tank size:** 45cm (18in).
**Tank region:** Mid to top.

## Breeding

Male guppies are sexually mature at three months and the females earlier than that. They breed readily and a good-sized female may produce 20-40 young. Feed the fry on crumbled flake food or tiny frozen and live foods. To reduce the risk of larger tankmates eating the young, add floating plants.

## Origins

*Central America to Brazil.*

*Males have a gonopodium – a modified anal fin with which they impregnate the female. The female has a normal-shaped anal fin.*

## Compatibility

*Take care with companions. The flowing finnage of the male guppies is tempting as a snack to other fish. Angels and tiger barbs are notorious for nipping the trailing fins and the damage they cause leaves open wounds that are susceptible to fungal attack.*

# SWORDTAIL ● *Xiphophorus helleri*

FAMILY: POECILIIDAE (LIVEBEARERS)

Swordtails are one of the mainstays of the aquarium trade. They have been bred to develop new colours and fin forms, but the red swordtail is still very popular. In good-quality fish, the colour is a rich blood-red and the male will not develop his sword until he is quite large. Avoid small fish that are already showing their swords, as these will not mature into good specimens to breed from. You will still be able to sex them by checking for the gonopodium in the male. Many colour forms are available, including red, black, green, half-black, wagtail (red with a black tail), albino and lyretail.

These active fish need plenty of swimming space, so confine the planting to the rear and sides of the aquarium. The fry also need plenty of room to grow, so avoid overcrowding them. They will feed by picking on algae and eating crumbled flake food.

## ◢ Breeding

Swordtails breed readily and can produce broods of as many as 80 fry, many of which will survive in the community aquarium provided there are some fine-leaved plants or floating plants for cover and no fish large enough to eat them!

## ◢ Ideal conditions

**Water:** Neutral, slightly hard.
**Temperature:** 21-28°C (70-82°F).
**Food:** Small live or frozen aquatic invertebrates, such as daphnia, mosquito larvae and bloodworm. Green foods. Flake foods.
**Minimum number in the aquarium:** One pair.
**Minimum tank size:** 90cm (36in).
**Tank region:** Mid to upper.

## ◢ Origins

*Central America.*

*Females are much deeper in the body and may show a gravid patch (a dark area near the vent indicating the presence of young fish yet to be released).*

**Left:** *Be sure to buy swordtails of the same colour forms as pairs, otherwise you will end up with some strange-looking cross-breeds in peculiar colours.*

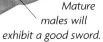

*Mature males will exhibit a good sword.*

# PLATY ● *Xiphophorus maculatus*

FAMILY: POECILIIDAE (LIVEBEARERS)

The platy is an excellent fish for the novice aquarist. It adapts well to aquarium life and makes a welcome, colourful addition to the community tank. The fish are peaceful, even with each other. Males can be distinguished from females by their gonopodium and, in mature fish, smaller size. They like to nibble at plants if insufficient green foods are offered, but do little damage, usually only taking algae from the leaves. Plant the tank with more robust plants, such as vallisneria, Amazon swordplants and Java fern.

Like its near relative, the swordtail, it has been developed to produce such well-known forms as red, wagtail, moon, tuxedo, blue hifin and sunset, to name but a few!

## Breeding

Platies will breed readily and even in the confines of the community tank, the fry can reach maturity. They are mature at about four months old and, fortunately, do not produce large broods. They are therefore much easier for the novice to cope with than the more prolific swordtail.

## Origins

Mexico, Guatemala and Northern Honduras.

*Red wagtail platies should have a blood red body and jet black fins.*

## Ideal conditions

**Water:** Neutral, slightly hard.
**Temperature:** 21-25°C (70-77°F).
**Food:** Small live or frozen aquatic invertebrates, such as daphnia, mosquito larvae and bloodworm. Green foods. Flake foods.
**Minimum number in the aquarium:** One pair.
**Minimum tank size:** 45cm (18in).
**Tank region:** Mid to upper.

*Left: Adult platies, being less than half the size of adult swordtails, make good community fish for those aquarists who only have space for a small aquarium.*

# SIAMESE FIGHTING FISH • *Betta splendens*

FAMILY: BELONTIIDAE (ANABANTIDS)

The highly coloured fish that are offered for sale today have been captive-bred to produce a wide variety of colours and extended finnage. The male is the flamboyant one with the long fins, the females are fairly dowdy with short fins.

Siamese fighting fish need warmth; aim to maintain a stable temperature, as fluctuations can cause stress and leave the fish open to infection. The other major cause of injury is keeping fighting fish with unsuitable companions that nip their trailing finnage. The damaged fins are then susceptible to fungal and bacterial attack.

Provide an aquarium with plants that not only reach the surface, but also grow in thickets that will provide a refuge for the fish.

## *Compatibility*

*You can keep a single male in one tank (other inmates permitting!) or even a male and several females, but do not keep two males together. These fish were originally bred for their belligerence and two males will fight, often to the death. The initial threat postures of spread gill covers and flared fins quickly develop into a series of attacks when the fish rip each other's fins.*

## Origins

*Thailand and Cambodia.*

*Healthy, happy fighters such as this one display their finnage to its best advantage.*

*Do not prevent these air-breathing fish from reaching the surface to take in air.*

## *Ideal conditions*

**Water:** Neutral, to slightly hard.
**Temperature:** 24-30°C (75-86°F).
**Food:** Small live or frozen aquatic invertebrates, such as daphnia, mosquito larvae and bloodworm. Flake foods.
**Minimum number in the aquarium:** Single male.
**Minimum tank size:** 45cm (18in).
**Tank region:** Top.

# DWARF GOURAMI ● *Colisa lalia*

FAMILY: BELONTIIDAE (ANABANTIDS)

These small gouramis are ideal for a peaceful community aquarium, but do not be tempted to add them to a new tank; wait a few months until things have settled down and stabilised before you contemplate buying them. Wild-caught fish are harder to acclimatise than their tank-bred counterparts. Fortunately, those offered for sale are tank-raised, so will settle better in your aquarium.

Buy a pair; in fact, they are usually sold this way. It is easy to tell the males from the females by their colour: females are more silvery, whereas males have red and blue bars along their bodies. Several colour forms are also available.

*When they are ready to spawn, females have a distended stomach.*

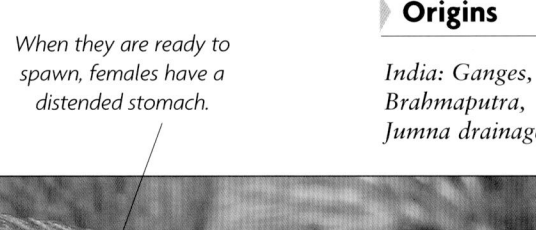

## Origins

India: Ganges, Brahmaputra, Jumna drainages.

## Ideal conditions

**Water:** Neutral, soft to slightly hard.
**Temperature:** 22-28°C (72-82°F).
**Food:** Small live or frozen aquatic invertebrates, such as daphnia, mosquito larvae and bloodworm. Flake foods.
**Minimum number in the aquarium:** One pair.
**Minimum tank size:** 45cm (18in).
**Tank region:** Middle to top.

**Health alert**
*Pay particular attention to water quality; if you forget a water change, the fish could be in trouble. If conditions do deteriorate, the fins may become ragged, the fish may go off their food and sulk in a quiet part of the tank. At worst, they may develop a bacterial infection.*

*Good males have unbroken red and blue bars on their sides.*

# PEARL GOURAMI • *Trichogaster leeri*

FAMILY: BELONTIIDAE (ANABANTIDS)

These beautiful fish are best kept in a larger community aquarium where they can swim and display to each other. Males have more intense colours and longer finnage than the females. It is safe to keep more than one male provided there is plenty of plant cover in the tank. The males may spar with each other but rarely do any real damage.

The pearl gourami is a hardy, long-lived species and an ideal fish for the novice aquarist. However, do not let the water temperature drop below the minimum given below. If the fish become chilled, at best they often go off their food and sulk, at worst they fall ill.

## Breeding

When breeding, the pair will build a bubblenest for the eggs and subsequent fry.

## Origins

*Thailand, Malaysia, Sumatra and Borneo.*

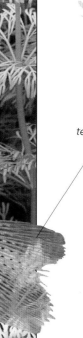

*The flowing fins are a great temptation to fin-nipping species and damaged fins can be affected by fungus.*

## Ideal conditions

**Water:** Neutral, to slightly hard.
**Temperature:** 24-28°C (75-82°F).
**Food:** They relish small live or frozen aquatic invertebrates, such as daphnia, mosquito larvae and bloodworm. Flake and green foods.
**Minimum number in the aquarium:** One pair.
**Minimum tank size:** 90cm (36in).
**Tank region:** Middle to top.

### Compatibility

*Choose companion species with care. Avoid any that may bully the gourami – cichlids are especially noted for their aggressive tendencies. In such situations, the gouramis refuse to eat, sulk in a corner and lose their colour.*

# BLUE GOURAMI or THREE-SPOT GOURAMI ● *Trichogaster trichopterus*

*Size: Males and females 10cm (4in)*

FAMILY: BELONTIIDAE (ANABANTIDS)

Because it is easy to keep and breed, this is a favourite fish among novice aquarists. The blue, or three-spot, gourami is one of the mainstays of the aquarium trade. It is also available in a gold and opaline form. The fish are omnivorous and will eat anything from flakes to flies.

Young fish are not always easy to sex but as they mature, the males develop a more pointed dorsal fin and their colour is a little more intense.

Blue gouramis are very useful in the aquarium because of their willingness to eat planarian worms, which saves you having to add any chemicals to the aquarium to eliminate these pests.

## Ideal conditions

**Water:** Neutral, to slightly hard.
**Temperature:** 22-28°C (72-82°F).
**Food:** Small live or frozen aquatic invertebrates, such as daphnia, mosquito larvae and bloodworm. Flake foods.
**Minimum number in the aquarium:** One pair.
**Minimum tank size:** 90cm (36in).
**Tank region:** Middle to top.

## Origins

*Southeast Asia: Burma, Thailand, Malaysia and Indonesia.*

The common name, three-spot, comes from the two spots on the body, plus the eye.

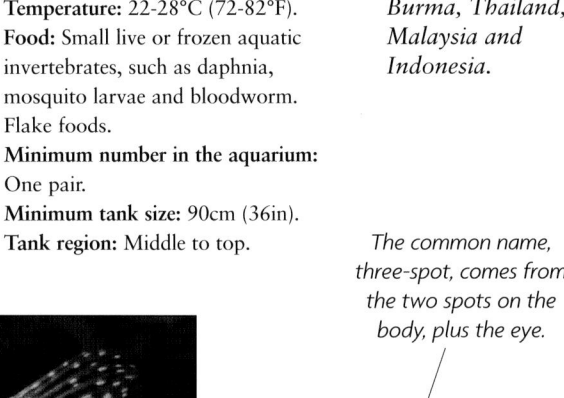

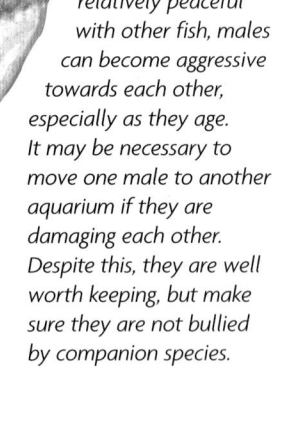

**Compatibility**
*Although they are relatively peaceful with other fish, males can become aggressive towards each other, especially as they age. It may be necessary to move one male to another aquarium if they are damaging each other. Despite this, they are well worth keeping, but make sure they are not bullied by companion species.*

# KISSING GOURAMI ● *Helostoma temmincki*

FAMILY: HELOSTOMATIDAE (ANABANTIDS)

A fish that is often kept just for the novelty of seeing the fish 'kiss'. However, the act has nothing to do with passion, but more with trials of strength to determine pecking order within a shoal or territorial boundaries. Despite this, they are a peaceable species that rarely do each other physical damage. The sexes are virtually impossible to distinguish.

Although the fish relish algae, you will need to feed them other foods, too. Offer flakes, frozen and also green foods. If you accustom them to eating frozen peas and some lettuce leaves, they will choose these in preference to your prized plants. To gain extra nourishment, these fish are also capable of filtering plankton through their gills.

To see them at their best, provide a spacious aquarium decorated with rocks, wood and broad-leaved plants. Keep the water clean and well filtered.

*In the wild, the kissing gourami is found in the poorly oxygenated waters of sluggish streams, swamps and pools. This is the pink form.*

## ▶ Ideal conditions

**Water:** Neutral, to slightly hard.
**Temperature:** 22-28°C (72-82°F).
**Food:** Small, live or frozen aquatic invertebrates, such as daphnia, mosquito larvae and bloodworm. Green foods and flake foods.
**Minimum number in the aquarium:** 1.
**Minimum tank size:** 90cm (36in).
**Tank region:** Middle to top.

*The green morph is less frequently available than the pink, but well worth keeping for its more subtle coloration.*

## ▶ Origins

*The green morph is found in Lake Bung Borapet in Thailand, while the pink morph occurs in Java.*

### Algae eaters

*In the aquarium, one of their greatest assets is the control of algae, especially in a new aquarium. It does not matter whether you buy the pink or the green form; a couple of youngsters added to a new set-up will happily go around the tank browsing on the algae. Although they eat vegetation, youngsters tend to eat the algae in preference to the plants, making them both useful and decorative. Their drawback is that they become quite large and may outgrow your aquarium.*

# BRONZE CORYDORAS • *Corydoras aeneus*

FAMILY: CALLICHTHYIDAE (MAILED, OR ARMOURED, CATFISHES)

*Corydoras aeneus* is ideal for the novice fishkeeper. It is easy to feed and like all the *Corydoras* species, but unlike some other catfish, active during the day. The fish dig into the substrate for food, so keep them in an aquarium with a fine rounded substrate, such as river sand or fine gravel, otherwise they could damage their delicate barbels. Although they dig, they do not uproot your plants. If you watch them carefully, they are sifting through the substrate as they would in the wild to find small worms and other tiny invertebrates.

Being a widespread species, the colour on *C. aeneus* can vary. It can also vary because the majority of the fish now available are captive-bred on fish farms. An albino form is also available.

## Breeding

The female holds two or three eggs in her cupped ventral fins while they are fertilised and then presses them onto a leaf. The fry grow rapidly if fed on newly hatched brine shrimp.

## Origins

*Trinidad and northern South America.*

### Compatibility

All Corydoras *species are shoaling fish that will happily shoal with other* Corydoras *species, so you need not keep them in single species groups.*

*A varied diet that includes live or frozen foods helps to keep the fish in good health and maintains the subtle greenish-bronze hues on the body.*

*Members of this family have two rows of bony plates along their sides.*

## Ideal conditions

**Water:** Slightly acidic to slightly alkaline, slightly soft to slightly hard.
**Temperature:** 22-26°C (72-79°F).
**Food:** Small live or frozen aquatic invertebrates, such as daphnia, mosquito larvae and bloodworm. Flake, tablet and granular food.
**Minimum number in the aquarium:** 2.
**Minimum tank size:** 60cm (24in).
**Tank region:** Bottom.

# PYGMY CORYDORAS ● *Corydoras hastatus*

FAMILY: CALLICHTHYIDAE (MAILED, OR ARMOURED, CATFISHES)

Pygmy corydoras are active throughout the day. These shoaling catfish like to swim about in midwater and rest on leaves and wood off the bottom of the tank. With habits such as these, they do not normally shoal with other *Corydoras* species, so you need to buy more of them. In the wild, small characins with a similar colour pattern to the corys are found within the shoal of catfish, presumably gaining some protection from the armoured catfish, whose spines make them an unsuitable meal for potential predators. *C. hastatus* is ideal for the smaller aquarium containing other small, peaceful fish.

Pygmy corydoras feed from the substrate, so it is important that this is fine; the fish are small and cannot sift through large grains of gravel. Offer them live or frozen as well as dried foods to keep them in good health.

## Breeding

These little corys are not easy to breed. They only produce 25-30 eggs and the tiny fry need a diet of infusoria (tiny ciliate animals) as a first food.

*Ideally, the planting in the tank should include a few broadleaved plants. Some flat stones and/or wood will also provide resting places where the fish can sit.*

## Origins

*The River Guapore in Brazil.*

## Ideal conditions

**Water:** Slightly acidic to slightly alkaline, slightly soft to slightly hard.
**Temperature:** 22-26°C (72-79°F).
**Food:** Small live or frozen aquatic invertebrates, such as daphnia, mosquito larvae and bloodworm. Tablet and granular foods. Flake foods once they sink to the bottom.
**Minimum number in the aquarium:** 6.
**Minimum tank size:** 45cm (18in).
**Tank region:** Bottom to middle.

# PORTHOLE CATFISH or DIANEMA • *Dianema longibarbis*

FAMILY: CALLICHTHYIDAE (MAILED, OR ARMOURED, CATFISHES)

Dianema are well-suited to the larger community aquarium stocked with medium-sized, peaceful fishes. They like plenty of swimming space and some open areas of substrate on which to feed. Like corydoras, to which they are related, they feed by sifting through the substrate. Make sure this is fine, with well-rounded grains, so that the fishes' delicate barbels and even their eyes are not damaged if they delve too deeply.

When buying your fish, look to see that they are active and that their fins, especially the caudal, are held out well. The first signs of their displeasure at deteriorating or inappropriate tank conditions are clamped fins, followed by degeneration of the barbels. Avoid fish showing these symptoms.

Dianema will eat most small foods, be they live, frozen or dried. They usually prefer feeding at dusk and dawn, so drop some tablet food into the tank just before you turn out the lights.

## ▶ Origins

*Peru, in the waters of the River Ambiacu.*

*In poor tank conditions or with inappropriate substrates, the barbels can be eroded or may degenerate and become susceptible to bacterial infection.*

## ▶ Breeding

This fish is rarely bred. It builds a bubblenest and the male, the slimmer of the pair, guards the eggs and fry.

*Barbels*

*Healthy fish show good colour and finnage.*

## ▶ Ideal conditions

**Water:** Slightly acidic to slightly alkaline, slightly soft to slightly hard.
**Temperature:** 22-26°C (72-79°F).
**Food:** Small live or frozen aquatic invertebrates, such as daphnia, mosquito larvae and bloodworm. Flake, tablet and sinking granules.
**Minimum number in the aquarium:** 2.
**Minimum tank size:** 90cm (36in).
**Tank region:** Bottom to middle.

# TALKING CATFISH ● *Amblydoras hancocki*

FAMILY: DORADIDAE (TALKING CATFISHES)

You can keep this peaceful catfish in the community aquarium provided you have no small fishes, such as small to medium-sized neon tetras, because the catfish is by nature a carnivore. These sedentary fish spend much of the day tucked away in a cave or a crevice in a piece of wood. In a planted tank, it is not unusual to see them resting among the plant leaves. Only in the evening do they venture out to feed.

These creatures are capable of making sounds. They can produce a low, rumbling growl by vibrating the swimbladder, and a more grating, rasping sound by moving a partially locked fin spine in its socket. It is a normal activity by which, we assume, the fish can communicate. It is most often heard when catching a fish, or if two are fighting over the same hollow in a piece of wood.

**Right:** *As the light fades, this catfish uses its sensitive barbels to find food on or in the substrate.*

### Safety first

*All doradids have a single row of scutes down their sides and stout fin spines. This armour makes them difficult to handle, as they can become entangled in nets. If this happens, put the fish and net back into the tank. The fish will often release itself, but if not, do not try to pull the net from the fish; instead, cut the net carefully away. Take care: catching a finger between a doradid's pectoral spine and the scutes is painful, especially if the fish is a large one!*

### ▶ Origins

*Guyana to Colombia.*

### ▶ *Ideal conditions*

**Water:** Slightly acidic to slightly alkaline, slightly soft to slightly hard.
**Temperature:** 22-28°C (72-82°F).
**Food:** Small live or frozen aquatic invertebrates, such as daphnia, mosquito larvae and bloodworm. Chopped meat foods, such as mussel. Tablet and sinking granular foods. May also take algae.
**Minimum number in the aquarium:** 1.
**Minimum tank size:** 60cm (24in).
**Tank region:** Bottom.

# BRISTLENOSE ● *Ancistrus sp.*

FAMILY: LORICARIIDAE (SUCKERMOUTH CATFISHES)

There are several species of *Ancistrus* that all look very similar. In the aquarium, their behaviour and needs are much the same. These little catfish will help to get rid of the algae that plagues every fishkeeper at some time, but it does not stop there. It will also eat the odd broadleaved plant if you do not feed it extra green foods, such as lettuce, courgettes and peas. Bristlenoses are constant grazers and we cannot grow sufficient algae in an aquarium to satisfy them, hence the need for additional foods.

Provide the fish with areas of shelter for the daytime and open areas of substrate that they can grub over during the hours of darkness. They like clean, clear, well-oxygenated water and should the oxygen levels fall – for example during extended hot weather – they will be found close to the water surface, where the oxygen levels are a little higher. A good external power filter with a spray bar return or additional aeration from an air pump will help alleviate such situations.

## Compatibility

*Bristlenoses are territorial and will squabble with other bottom-dwelling fish, as well as with each other if you try to crowd them.*

## Origins

*Tropical South America.*

*Males have large bushy bristles on and around the head; females just have a row of very fine bristles around the snout.*

## Ideal conditions

**Water:** Slightly acidic to neutral, soft to slightly hard.
**Temperature:** 22-27°C (72-80°F).
**Food:** Green foods, plus small aquatic invertebrates, especially frozen bloodworm. May take flake and tablet foods.
**Minimum number in the aquarium:** One pair.
**Minimum tank size:** 90cm (36in).
**Tank region:** Bottom.

# OTOCINCLUS ● *Otocinclus affinis*

FAMILY: LORICARIIDAE (SUCKERMOUTH CATFISHES)

This small catfish likes a well-planted aquarium and small, peaceful companions. Like other loricariids, it has stout fin spines and three rows of bony plates along its body for protection. Beware when handling the fish, as they may become entangled in the net. Do not attempt to pull a fish free; either let it free itself or carefully cut away the net.

Remember that this creature is for the most part herbivorous. It is one of the best algae eaters for the aquarium, but it is very rare for an aquarium to provide enough algae to satisfy its needs. You must therefore provide plenty of green foods in the diet. The easiest way is to offer frozen peas or to 'plant' lettuce leaves in the substrate for the fish to graze over. Do remove the old leaves and peas before they start to decompose.

Otocinclus are not happy if the water conditions begin to deteriorate. They go off their food and may hang near the surface. Regular water changes and efficient filtration should help avoid this situation.

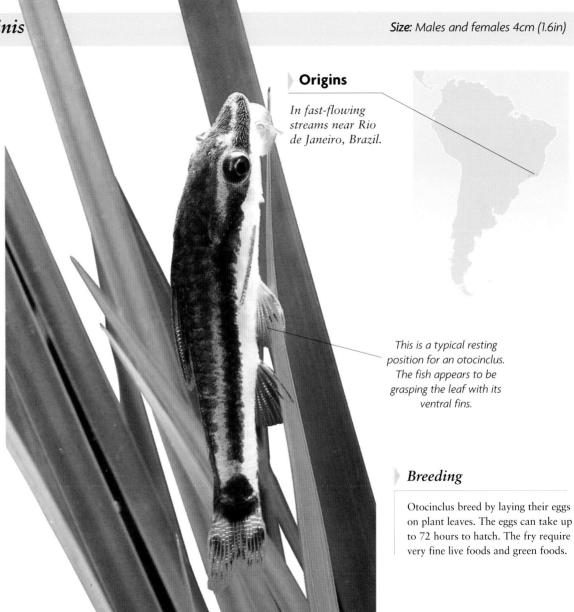

## Origins

*In fast-flowing streams near Rio de Janeiro, Brazil.*

*This is a typical resting position for an otocinclus. The fish appears to be grasping the leaf with its ventral fins.*

## Ideal conditions

**Water:** Slightly acidic to slightly alkaline, slightly soft to slightly hard.
**Temperature:** 20-26°C (68-79°F).
**Food:** Flake and tablet food. Algae and green foods.
**Minimum number in the aquarium:** 2.
**Minimum tank size:** 45cm (18in).
**Tank region:** Bottom to middle.

## Breeding

Otocinclus breed by laying their eggs on plant leaves. The eggs can take up to 72 hours to hatch. The fry require very fine live foods and green foods.

# BUTTERFLY PLEC ● *Peckoltia pulcher*

FAMILY: LORICARIIDAE (SUCKERMOUTH CATFISH)

This is one little loricariid catfish that does not cause too much trouble in the community aquarium. For most of the day it lurks beneath a stone or under plants, but in the evening you will see it rummaging around the aquarium in search of its favourite food – algae. Now, no matter how hard you try, the tank can never grow enough algae to keep it happy, so be sure to provide alternatives in the form of lettuce, frozen peas, courgettes and potato.

P. pulcher requires clean water with a reasonable oxygen content. It makes no demands on its companions, as it tends to keep itself to itself. Despite being a herbivore, it also leaves the plants alone, neither digging them up nor eating them. Little is known of its breeding habits.

## Ideal conditions

**Water:** Slightly acidic to neutral, soft to slightly hard.
**Temperature:** 23-28°C (73-82°F).
**Food:** Green foods, plus small aquatic invertebrates, especially frozen bloodworm. May take flake and tablet foods.
**Minimum number in the aquarium:** 1.
**Minimum tank size:** 60cm (24in).
**Tank region:** Bottom.

## Compatibility

*This otherwise faultless fish does have one drawback: it is quarrelsome with its own kind, especially if there is not enough room for each one to have its own territory or there are insufficient hiding places. Since their territory is just the substrate, keep only one fish in a 60x30cm (24x12in) tank. However, in a 90cm (36in) tank that is 38 or 45cm (15 or 18in) wide, you could probably keep two.*

## Origins

*South America: in the waters of the Rivers Negro, Xingu and Madeira.*

# LANCEOLATE WHIPTAIL ● *Rineloricaria lanceolata*

*Size:* Males and females 12cm (4.7in)

FAMILY: LORICARIIDAE (SUCKERMOUTH CATFISHES)

This is probably one of the easiest whiptails to identify because of its coloration and the broad dark mark in the front part of the dorsal fin. The fish prefer an aquarium that is set up with broadleaved plants and wood, where they can find caves and hollows to rest in. Unlike many other species of whiptail, which seek shelter on the substrate, they are often seen resting up among the plants. A gentle current of water through the aquarium is beneficial, as this keeps the oxygen levels high. The fish do not like still water.

Although they feed on plant matter, they do little damage to aquarium plants provided you feed them lettuce and peas, etc. Do not forget to take out the uneaten food before it pollutes the tank.

## Breeding

As the fish mature, the males develop bristles on the sides of the head. These become more prominent when they are ready to spawn, but even at other times you can detect fine bristles if you look carefully or gently feel the cheeks with your finger. When the females are ready to breed, they become much deeper in the body as their abdomen fills with eggs. The eggs are laid in hollows or caves and are guarded by the parents. The fry can be difficult to raise.

## Ideal conditions

**Water:** Slightly acidic to slightly alkaline, slightly soft to slightly hard.
**Temperature:** 21-26°C (70-79°F).
**Food:** Small live or frozen aquatic invertebrates, such as daphnia, mosquito larvae and bloodworm. Flake and green foods.
**Minimum number in the aquarium:** 2.
**Minimum tank size:** 60cm (24in).
**Tank region:** Bottom to middle.

## Origins

*South America: Ecuador, Peru, Brazil, Bolivia and Paraguay.*

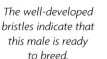

*The well-developed bristles indicate that this male is ready to breed.*

# ROYAL WHIPTAIL or ROYAL FARLOWELLA • *Sturisoma panamense*

FAMILY: LORICARIIDAE (SUCKERMOUTH CATFISH)

The stunning royal whiptail is well worth keeping if you have a larger, well-established community aquarium with fish that will not pick at the catfish's trailing finnage. It is not suitable for a newly set up tank.

To keep the fish healthy, pay particular attention to maintaining water quality. It should be well filtered, with a high oxygen content. They will graze on green food, as well as taking commercially prepared foods that sink, and frozen and live bloodworm and daphnia – yes, even these bottom dwellers are partial to daphnia and are comical to watch while catching it!

Keep them in a tank with open areas of substrate for them to feed over. They will also rasp over wood and plants but, provided you give them enough alternative green foods, they do little, if any, damage to plants.

### Ideal conditions

**Water:** Slightly acidic to slightly alkaline, slightly soft to slightly hard.
**Temperature:** 22-27°C (72-80°F).
**Food:** Small live or frozen aquatic invertebrates, such as daphnia, mosquito larvae and bloodworm. Flake food. Algae and green foods.
**Minimum number in the aquarium:** One pair.
**Minimum tank size:** 90cm (36in).
**Tank region:** Bottom to middle.

*Males have cheek bristles during the breeding season and are generally slimmer than females when viewed from above.*

### Origins

*Central America: Panama.*

### Breeding

The fish will breed in captivity, often laying their eggs on the aquarium glass. The male guards and cleans the eggs. The fry require very tiny foods such as infusoria (tiny ciliate animals).

*The fish have long whiptail extensions to their caudal fin and use these as feelers to detect food items by bending the caudal fin to the side and forwards.*

# UPSIDE-DOWN CATFISH ● *Synodontis nigriventris*

**Size:** Males 7.5cm (3in), females 10cm (4in)

FAMILY: MOCHOKIDAE (UPSIDE-DOWN CATFISHES)

The upside-down catfish is always a talking point because of its way of swimming. In the wild, it is found beneath floating logs and vegetation, where it swims inverted, feeding on insects that land on the water surface and on prey items, such as mosquito larvae. Its coloration is suited to its life style. The belly is dark brown so that passing predators, such as birds, cannot easily see it when they look into the water, while its back is a much lighter brown, so that when seen by predators in the water beneath it, it blends into the logs and plants debris. Most active at dawn and dusk, it can be tempted out at almost any time by food. It will take flake food from the surface and is not averse to turning up the right way and taking a pellet or tablet from the substrate!

These peaceful creatures are quite at home in the community aquarium.

**Health check**
*If there is a problem with the water, the barbels will begin to degenerate. If this happens, do a water change and check that the filtration system is working properly.*

## Breeding

These fish have been captive bred. Males are slimmer and smaller than females. The best natural food to bring them into spawning condition is mosquito larvae. The eggs are deposited in a depression in the substrate and both parents care for the eggs and fry.

## Origins

*Central Africa: Zaire Basin.*

*In the aquarium it is happy with plants that reach to the surface and wood that arches over to provide a retreat.*

## Ideal conditions

**Water:** Slightly acidic to slightly alkaline, slightly soft to slightly hard.
**Temperature:** 22-26°C (72-79°F).
**Food:** Small live or frozen aquatic invertebrates, such as daphnia, mosquito larvae and bloodworm. Flake food.
**Minimum number in the aquarium:** 2.
**Minimum tank size:** 60cm (24in).
**Tank region:** Middle to top.

63

# GLASS CATFISH ● *Kryptopterus bicirrhis*

**Size:** *Males and females 13cm (5in)*

FAMILY: SILURIDAE (SHEAT CATFISHES)

Catfish are often the last to be considered for a community aquarium because it is mistakenly believed that they are scavengers and therefore not very interesting. Nothing could be further from the truth with the glass catfish. These midwater shoaling fish are active during the day, feeding in the same manner as tetras and barbs. And they have an added attraction: you can see right through them! The silvery sac at the front of the fish houses its delicate organs, while the transparent body allows you to view the spine and fin rays with ease. You can even see the plants behind them! Despite their bizarre appearance, they are not too difficult to keep. Be sure to maintain the water quality and provide them with a reasonable flow of water through the tank (they like to swim in this). Keep a minimum of four fish; single specimens feel insecure, will hide away, refuse to eat and may die. At rest, the fish hang at an angle, but when swimming they are horizontal.

*When swimming, glass catfish are horizontal. When they are at rest they hang tail down, their bodies at an angle.*

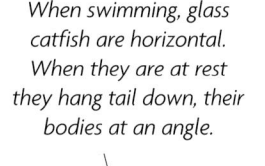

## ▶ Breeding

Little is known of their breeding, although there are reports of accidental spawnings when fry have just appeared in the aquarium. The fry were then raised on infusoria followed by daphnia.

## ▶ Origins

*Eastern India, Thailand, Malaysia and Indonesia.*

### Compatibility

*Keep these peaceful fish with tankmates of 4cm (1.6in) or more. Good-sized glass catfish may eat fry or even small neons.*

## ▶ Ideal conditions

**Water:** Slightly acidic to slightly alkaline, slightly soft to slightly hard.
**Temperature:** 21-26°C (70-79°F).
**Food:** Small live or frozen aquatic invertebrates, such as daphnia, mosquito larvae and bloodworm. Flake food.
**Minimum number in the aquarium:** 4.
**Minimum tank size:** 60cm (24in).
**Tank region:** Middle to top.

# LOACH ● *Botia lohachata*

FAMILY: COBITIDAE (LOACHES)

Although *Botia lohachata* is a nocturnal fish, it is easily attracted out at other times by the offer of food. The best time to feed the fish is at twilight, when they will rummage in the substrate and even take flake food from the surface. Use a fine substrate in the tank to prevent any damage to their barbels when foraging.

The small, erectile spine below the eye (the bifid spine) is used defensively if the fish feels threatened. Loaches are relatively hardy fish, provided you remember to carry out regular water changes. Live or frozen foods bring out the best coloration. Although they can be kept alone, they can also be combined with other small botia species, provided your aquarium is large enough.

## ▶ Ideal conditions

**Water:** Neutral, slightly hard.
**Temperature:** 24-30°C (75-86°F).
**Food:** Small live or frozen aquatic invertebrates, such as daphnia, mosquito larvae and bloodworm. Tablet foods. Flake foods.
**Minimum number in the aquarium:** 1.
**Minimum tank size:** 60cm (24in).
**Tank region:** Bottom to midwater.

## ▶ Origins

*Northeastern India and Bangladesh.*

**Compatibility**

*Loaches can be aggressive, especially if several other bottom-dwelling fish are competing for the available substrate space. They will defend their territory, using their bifid spines to scratch the bodies of the other fish.*

*The colour pattern on this loach can vary quite considerably.*

*When the fish are fighting or frightened, you can hear clicking sounds produced by the raising and lowering of the bifid spine.*

# CHAIN LOACH or DWARF LOACH • *Botia sidthimunki*

FAMILY: COBITIDAE (LOACHES)

Chain, or dwarf, loaches are peaceful, active fish that are out and about during the day. Be sure to keep them as a group so that they can interact with each other. Although they are predominantly bottom-dwelling fish, you can often see them resting on the leaves of broadleaved plants such as Amazon swordplants. Provide a fine substrate so that they can dig for small items of food without causing any discernible damage to the decor! Before adding chain loaches to the tank, wait until the water has had time to mature properly – three to six months – as these fish suffer when placed in a newly set-up system. To keep them healthy, remember to carry out regular water changes.

## ▶ Breeding

There are no obvious sexual differences and there is no available breeding information.

## ▶ Origins

*Northern parts of India and Thailand.*

*Botia have a small spine below the eye (the bifid spine), which they can erect and lower at will as a form of defence. When they use the spine, they sometimes produce an audible clicking sound.*

## ▶ Ideal conditions

**Water:** Neutral to slightly acidic, slightly hard.
**Temperature:** 25-28°C (77-82°F).
**Food:** Small live or frozen aquatic invertebrates, such as daphnia, mosquito larvae and bloodworm. Tablet foods and flake food (once it has fallen to the bottom).
**Minimum number in the aquarium:** 6.
**Minimum tank size:** 60cm (24in).
**Tank region:** Bottom to midwater.

# COOLIE LOACH ● *Pangio kuhlii*

FAMILY: COBITIDAE (LOACHES)

Coolies are more active at night. They spend the day hidden among plant roots or in nooks and crannies, but come out to feed in the early evening when the light starts to fade. If you provide shady areas in the aquarium (use broadleaved plants) coolies will feel safe and readily come out to feed.

These long, slim fish are very adept at getting beneath undergravel filter plates and up the intake pipes to external filters. There is virtually nothing you can do about this and the fish manage to get out as easily as they got in. Make sure you always use a basket over power filter intakes and be sure to check what is in the bottom of the filter bucket before you throw out the debris!

Use a fine substrate, as coolies like to bury into it and coarse gravel can damage their bodies. This annoying habit can make catching coolies quite a challenge.

## Ideal conditions

**Water:** Slightly hard, slightly acidic.
**Temperature:** 24-28°C (75-82°F).
**Food:** Small live or frozen aquatic invertebrates, such as daphnia, mosquito larvae or bloodworm. Tablet foods and flake food (once it has fallen to the bottom).
**Minimum number in the aquarium:** 1 (but two is better).
**Minimum tank size:** 60cm (24in).
**Tank region:** Bottom.

## Origins

*Southeast Asia: Thailand, Malaysia, Singapore, Sumatra, Java and Borneo.*

## Breeding

Coolies have been bred in captivity. They lay bright green eggs that stick to the leaves, stems and roots of floating plants.

*When catching coolies, try using two nets, one held still against the substrate and the side of the tank, the other to guide the fish along gently.*

# CAPE LOPEZ LYRETAIL • *Aphyosemion australe*

***Size:** Males and females 6cm (2.4in)*

FAMILY: APLOCHEILIDAE (KILLIFISHES)

Although not often considered for the community aquarium, you can keep these colourful killifish with other small, peaceful species that require similar tank conditions. However, it is best not to combine them with other *Aphyosemion* species because the females of each species can look much the same and, should you wish to breed them, you will not be able to tell them apart. There is also the possibility that the species may interbreed. Provide plenty of shelter in the aquarium using fine-leaved plants and one or two floating plants.

The filtration system should provide a very gentle water turnover. These fish cannot tolerate poor quality water, so take care not to overfeed them, as uneaten foods quickly pollute the aquarium.

The brilliantly coloured males are popular, but the fish are usually sold in pairs or sometimes trios. Males display ceaselessly to the females. Despite popular myths that they are short-lived, these killifish can live for up to three years.

## Breeding

The fish hang their eggs by a thread on plants and can be encouraged to use a spawning mop in the aquarium. They produce between 10 and 20 eggs daily. You can remove the mop full of eggs to a separate tank to hatch and add a new mop.

## Ideal conditions

**Water:** Slightly acidic, soft.
**Temperature:** 21-24°C (70-75°F).
**Food:** The fish prefer small live foods, but quickly adapt to the frozen equivalent. Offer flake foods, too.
**Minimum number in the aquarium:** Pair or trio (1 male, 2 females).
**Minimum tank size:** 45cm (18in).
**Tank region:** Lower to midwater.

## Origins

*Cameroon, Gabon and Congo.*

### Safety first

*Be sure to use a cover glass; these fish jump!*

*Other fish will quickly nip off the fin extensions unless companions are chosen with care.*

# SPARKLING PANCHAX ● *Aplocheilus lineatus*

FAMILY: APLOCHEILIDAE (KILLIFISHES)

You can tell that this fish lives at the water surface just by looking at its body shape. The back is flat and straight, with the dorsal fin set well back so that it does not break the water surface and betray the fish's presence to any predatory birds. The mouth is right at the front of the head and is slightly upturned – ideal for feeding from the surface.

If you are looking for a surface-dwelling fish, the sparkling panchax may just fit the bill. It is not too fussy about the water condition as long as it is not too hard. However, do not overlook regular water changes, otherwise the fish may suffer from bacterial infections. An aquarium with open water and plants to the sides and rear is suitable. Some of the plants should reach up to the water surface to provide some shelter for the fish.

## Ideal conditions

**Water:** Neutral to slightly hard.
**Temperature:** 22-25°C (72-77°F).
**Food:** If possible, feed small live and frozen foods. Live mosquito larvae are a particular favourite and will bring the fish into spawning condition. If these are not available, the fish will eagerly take frozen bloodworm, but not once it has fallen to the substrate. Offer flake as a supplement.
**Minimum number in the aquarium:** Pair or trio (1 male, 2 females).
**Minimum tank size:** 60cm (24in).
**Tank region:** Top.

## Origins

*Central and southern India.*

### Safety first

*If frightened, the sparkling panchax's immediate reaction is to jump, so be sure to use a cover glass!*

## Breeding

*A. lineatus* lays its eggs on fine-leaved plants and/or spawning mops, which you can remove to another container for hatching. The eggs take up to two weeks to hatch and the fry need very fine live foods.

### Compatibility

*Can be aggressive with its own kind, so just keep a pair or trio unless you have a large aquarium (120cm/48in or more), which would allow the fish space to get away from each other. They are also predatory and will eat smaller fish and especially fry, so keep them with other similar-sized fish.*

FAMILY: MELANOTAENIIDAE (RAINBOWFISHES)

One of the larger rainbowfish, *Melanotaenia boesemani*, is an active fish that requires a good-sized aquarium with plenty of open water to swim in. Although it likes clean, clear water, a strong water flow is not essential; a gentle current from a power filter will suffice.

When buying these fish, make sure that you acquire both males and females. This is easy to ascertain in adults, as the males have beautiful blue and yellow coloration. It is best to buy young stock and allow them to pair off themselves. Bear in mind that when these fish have been tank-bred for several generations, the intensity of colour diminishes in each successive generation. Feeding large amounts of live or frozen foods such as bloodworm helps to maintain the sheen on the fish.

### Compatibility

*Boeseman's rainbowfish are quite at home with other fish of a similar size and nature, especially if their companions are not shoaling fish and therefore occupying the same water region of the aquarium.*

### ▶ Origins

*Ajamaru Lakes, Irian Jaya.*

*When mature, the males develop a much deeper body and the head becomes more pointed.*

*To maintain the beautiful sheen on the body, feed the fish mostly on live and/or frozen foods.*

### ▶ Ideal conditions

**Water:** Slightly acid, soft to slightly hard.
**Temperature:** 24-30°C (75-86°F).
**Food:** Small live or frozen aquatic invertebrates, such as daphnia, mosquito larvae and bloodworm. Flake foods.
**Minimum number in the aquarium:** 4.
**Minimum tank size:** 90cm (36in).
**Tank region:** Midwater.

### Caution

*Make sure you use a cover glass on the aquarium as these fish can sometimes jump.*

FAMILY: MELANOTAENIIDAE (RAINBOWFISHES)

The prime reason for keeping this delightful rainbowfish is its brilliant blue coloration. Males are much more colourful than females, but you need to keep both so that the males have something to display to. They are very active fish and need space, so plant the aquarium towards the sides and back to allow the rainbows room to move. Keep them with similar-sized companions; as adults they are not averse to eating very small fish, such as young neons. Make sure you use a cover glass, as they will often jump if frightened. Feeding rainbowfish is simple; if it fits in their mouths, they eat it. Flake, freeze-dried, frozen and live foods are all avidly consumed.

### Water conditions

*Water conditions play a large part in the fishes' well-being. Make sure that the filtration system is working efficiently and that there is a gentle current through the tank. Carry out regular water changes; if the water deteriorates, the fins will start to look ragged at the edges, as though they have been nibbled by other fish. A water change should solve the problem.*

### ▶ Origins

*Lake Kutubu in Papua New Guinea.*

### ▶ *Ideal conditions*

**Water:** Slightly acidic to neutral, soft to slightly hard.
**Temperature:** 23-30°C (73-86°F).
**Food:** Small live or frozen aquatic invertebrates, such as daphnia, mosquito larvae and bloodworm. Flake foods. Green foods.
**Minimum number in the aquarium:** One pair.
**Minimum tank size:** 90cm (36in).
**Tank region:** Middle to top.

*These lively fish can sometimes damage their fins and bodies if they jump and collide with sharp objects in the tank.*

### ▶ *Breeding*

Rainbowfish lay their eggs over a period of days. They are quite easy to breed but it is not as easy to raise the fry. Large amounts of tiny live foods are required for this.

# DWARF NEON RAINBOWFISH • *Melanotaenia praecox*

FAMILY: MELANOTAENIIDAE (RAINBOWFISHES)

This little rainbowfish is a joy to keep. It is undemanding as far as water conditions are concerned, providing you avoid the extremes of hardness and pH. Keep a minimum of six of these peaceful, shoaling fish in the aquarium, but to see them at their best, house 10 or more in a well-planted aquarium with plenty of swimming space. In the wild, they are found in streams and benefit from a gentle flow of water through the aquarium. Ensure that the filtration system is efficient and remember to carry out regular water changes.

Adults are bright blue in colour, which contrasts well with their red fins. To help maintain their coloration, feed them well with live and frozen foods, such as mosquito larvae and bloodworm.

## Breeding

Well-fed adults will lay large quantities of eggs over Java moss. If adults remain well nourished, you can leave the eggs and fry in the same tank. However, if you keep other species in the aquarium, remove the eggs, as other fish will quickly polish off the fry. The young do not start to develop their blue coloration until they are about 2.5cm (1in) long.

## Origins

*Mamberamo River, northern Irian Jaya, New Guinea.*

*This beautiful male fish would make ideal breeding stock.*

## Ideal conditions

**Water:** Slightly acid, slightly soft to slightly hard.
**Temperature:** 24-27°C (75-80°F).
**Food:** Small live or frozen aquatic invertebrates, such as daphnia, mosquito larvae and bloodworm. Flake foods.
**Minimum number in the aquarium:** 6.
**Minimum tank size:** 60cm (24in).
**Tank region:** Midwater.

FAMILY: ELEOTRIDAE (GOBIES)

Some gobies grow large and belligerent, so they are not often considered for inclusion in a community aquarium. However, one small species, the peacock goby, is ideal for adding to a well-balanced planted aquarium that has been set-up for six months or more. Its brightly patterned body makes it an obvious choice on the grounds of colour alone, but add to that its peaceful nature and it should be a firm favourite.

The fish are usually sold as pairs. Males are more highly coloured, have larger finnage and are slimmer than the females. Females sport almost the same colouring, but the belly is more rounded and lighter in colour and the finnage much shorter. The fish are easy to feed but prefer small live foods or their frozen equivalents.

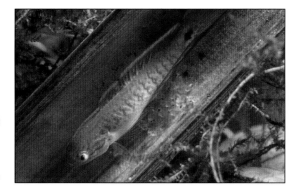

*Below: The pair clean a firm substrate on which to place the eggs. The male guards the eggs, fanning them to keep a good supply of oxygenated water over them.*

### ▶ Origins

*Papua New Guinea.*

#### Compatibility

*Do not keep these gentle fish with larger species that will bully them, otherwise the gobies will hide away and refuse to feed.*

*If the fish is unhappy with the water conditions, the fins can appear slightly ragged at the edges.*

### ▶ Ideal conditions

**Water:** Neutral, soft.
**Temperature:** 22-26°C (72-79°F).
**Food:** Small live or frozen aquatic invertebrates, such as daphnia, mosquito larvae and bloodworm. Flake foods.
**Minimum number in the aquarium:** One pair.
**Minimum tank size:** 60cm (24in).
**Tank region:** Lower.

*Plenty of live and/or frozen foods will help to maintain the fishes' brilliant colours.*

# KEYHOLE CICHLID • *Cleithracara maronii*

FAMILY: CICHLIDAE (CICHLIDS)

Keyhole cichlids are delightful, peaceful little fish that adapt well to the community aquarium, where their delicate coloration contrasts well with more flamboyant species. Their digging is confined to the breeding season and even then they do little damage and do not uproot plants. They can be nervous and if frightened, their coloration becomes mottled brown. Provide them with sheltered areas where they can hide if they feel threatened.

In the wild, these fish grow much larger than tank-bred ones, but wild-caught specimens are not often available; when they are, they are much sought after and command high prices. Keyholes have been commercially bred for generations and the stocks available now do not grow as large as their wild ancestors.

## Ideal conditions

**Water:** Slightly acid to slightly alkaline, slightly hard.
**Temperature:** 22-25°C (72-77°F).
**Food:** Small live or frozen aquatic invertebrates, such as daphnia, mosquito larvae and bloodworm. Flake foods.
**Minimum number in the aquarium:** One pair.
**Minimum tank size:** 60cm (24in).
**Tank region:** Lower to midwater.

## Origins

*Southern Venezuela and Guyana in slow-moving rivers and streams.*

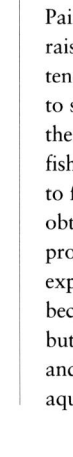
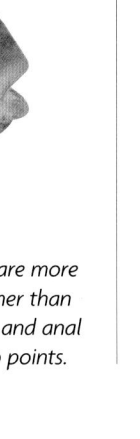

Adult males are more colourful and slimmer than females. Their dorsal and anal fins are extended to points.

## Breeding

Pairs establish their territory and will raise a family, with both parents tending the fry. When they are ready to spawn, females can be identified by their deeper, rounded bodies. Young fish will not be sexable, so buy three to five to increase the chance of obtaining a pair. A mature pair can produce up to 300 fry, but do not expect to raise all of them. Some will become food for other tank inmates, but quite a proportion will survive and you may need to set up another aquarium to grow them on.

# ANGELFISH ● *Pterophyllum scalare*

FAMILY: CICHLIDAE (CICHLIDS)

Angels are majestic fish, beloved of many aquarists. Most commercially available fish are tank-bred and many exhibit symptoms of inbreeding, such as poor colour and stunted growth, but the most significant factor is the inability of some of these fish to behave normally as cichlid parents. They have no idea what to do with their eggs or fry and it is generally believed that this is due to the practice of removing the eggs from the parents to hatch and raise the fry separately and thus ensure a much larger brood than normal.

The sexes are not easy to distinguish and the only reliable way is to look at the short breeding tube that extends from the vent. In males it is pointed, in females, rounded. Buy young fish and grow them up in a planted aquarium. Provide open water in the centre, with broadleaved plants, such as Amazon swordplants, and thickets of vallisneria at the sides and back. If you wish, add some low-growing plants in the centre.

### Safety first

*Only keep angelfish with fish they cannot eat. A half-grown angelfish will consume small neons!*

### Origins

*Central Amazon River and its tributaries, into Peru and eastern Ecuador.*

### Compatibility

*As youngsters the fish are peaceful, but as they pair off, they can become territorial, especially towards other angelfish. At this point, it is a good idea to remove the other angelfish and just keep this pair in the aquarium. Although they will dominate other species in the aquarium, they do not usually cause any actual bodily harm.*

*Angelfish have been bred to create several colour morphs (gold, black, half-black, etc.) and fin forms (veiltail and lace). While the colour forms are reasonably robust, those with extended finnage require higher temperatures and good water quality and can be quite difficult to keep.*

### Ideal conditions

**Water:** Slightly acidic to neutral, slightly soft to slightly hard.
**Temperature:** 24-28°C (75-82°F).
**Food:** Angelfish are greedy and will eat small live foods, frozen and flake foods to excess. This can result in their early demise. Do not overfeed.
**Minimum number in the aquarium:** 3-4.
**Minimum tank size:** 90cm (36in).
**Tank region:** Midwater.

# GOLDEN DWARF ACARA ● *Nannacara anomala*

FAMILY: CICHLIDAE (CICHLIDS)

The males of this species are very easy to distinguish, as they are much larger and far more highly coloured than the females. They are usually sold as pairs so that the dealer is not left with all the drab females. By keeping a pair, you can be sure that the male will nearly always look his best in order to keep the attention of his partner.

Golden dwarf acara are quite at home in a well-planted community aquarium, with caves for shelter and a fine substrate to accommodate their digging. However, when they start breeding, they may assume territorial rights over the whole aquarium, herding the other fish into one part and making sure that they remain there. Fortunately, they seldom do any harm to the other fish.

These fish prefer small live and frozen foods and will only accept flakes grudgingly. Check to see what the dealer has been feeding them and do likewise.

## Ideal conditions

**Water:** Slightly acidic, slightly hard.
**Temperature:** 22-25°C (72-77°F).
**Food:** Small live or frozen aquatic invertebrates, such as daphnia, mosquito larvae and bloodworm. Flake foods.
**Minimum number in the aquarium:** One pair.
**Minimum tank size:** 60cm (24in).
**Tank region:** Bottom to midwater.

## ▶ Breeding

The fish spawn in a cave. After spawning, the female takes charge of the eggs and subsequent fry, while the male defends the territory against allcomers.

## ▶ Origins

*Guyana, in the River Essequibo.*

*The dorsal and anal fins of the male are extended to a point.*

*Two males will often spar with each other and may even fight.*

# KRIBENSIS or PURPLE CICHLID • *Pelvicachromis pulcher*

FAMILY: CICHLIDAE (CICHLIDS)

The attractive kribensis is a very good choice for the novice fishkeeper. Wild-caught fish are rarely imported (and expensive when they are) so the commercially raised, tank-bred fish are acclimatised to life in the average community aquarium. When you buy them, watch the tank for a while and you should be able to distinguish males from females. If you are really lucky, you may even acquire two that have already established a pair bond.

Kribensis will feel at home in a well-planted community aquarium, especially if you provide some caves that can be used as possible spawning sites. For the most part they are peaceful, and although they may dig in the substrate, they do not uproot the plants. Make sure you provide a fine substrate to allow for digging, as this activity is an essential part of the breeding ritual for many species of cichlid. They are easy to feed, taking just about anything that will fit into their mouths.

*Males are slightly larger and their dorsal and anal fins are pointed, while the caudal fin has extended rays in the central portion.*

### ▶ Origins

*Southern Nigeria, mostly west of the River Niger.*

*The smaller female is brightly coloured and has a bright pink belly when ready to spawn. Her fins are rounded.*

### ▶ *Ideal conditions*

**Water:** Slightly acidic, medium hard.
**Temperature:** 24-25°C (75-77°F).
**Food:** Small live or frozen aquatic invertebrates, such as daphnia, mosquito larvae and bloodworm. Flake foods.
**Minimum number in the aquarium:** One pair.
**Minimum tank size:** 60cm (24in).
**Tank region:** Bottom to midwater.

# INDEX

Page numbers in **bold** indicate major entries; *italics* refer to captions and annotations; plain type indicates other text entries.

## CREDITS

The publishers would like to thank the following photographers for providing images, credited here by page number and position: B(Bottom), T(Top), C(Centre), BL(Bottom Left), etc.

David Allison: 12(C)

MP & C Piednoir/Aqua Press - France: Copyright page, Contents page (T), 8, 12(B), 14, 16, 17, 18, 23(B), 25(T), 32, 34, 39, 41, 42(T,B), 43(C,B), 44(C,B) 45, 46(C,B), 48, 49, 50(C,BR), 51, 52(BL), 53(T), 56, 59, 61, 64, 67, 70(C,B), 71, 73(T,B), 77(C,B)

Photomax (Max Gibbs): Title page, 13, 15, 19, 20, 21, 22, 24, 26, 27, 28, 33, 35, 36, 37, 47, 53(B), 55, 58, 60, 63, 65, 66, 72, 74, 76

Mike Sandford: Contents (B), 7, 9, 29, 30, 31, 38(L,R), 52(BR), 54, 57, 62, 68, 75

Iggy Tavares: 23(C), 40

W A Tomey: 25(B), 69

Thanks are due to Morden Water World, Surrey SM4 5JG, England, for their help during the preparation of this book.

The information and recommendations in this book are given without any guarantees on the part of the author and publisher, who disclaim any liability with the use of this material.